THE COMMON CORE STATE STANI

A series designed to help educators successfully
implement CCSS literacy standards in K–12 classrooms

SUSAN B. NEUMAN AND D. RAY REUTZEL, EDITORS
SERIES BOARD: Diane August, Linda Gambrell, Steve Graham, Laura Justice,
Margaret McKeown, and Timothy Shanahan

Professional Learning in Action
An Inquiry Approach for Teachers of Literacy
VICTORIA J. RISKO & MARYELLEN VOGT

Young Meaning Makers—Teaching Comprehension, Grades K–2
D. RAY REUTZEL, SARAH K. CLARK, CINDY D. JONES, & SANDRA L. GILLAM

Revitalizing Read Alouds
Interactive Talk About Books with Young Children, PreK–2
LISA HAMMETT PRICE & BARBARA A. BRADLEY

RTI in the Common Core Classroom
A Framework for Instruction and Assessment
SHARON VAUGHN, PHILIP CAPIN, GARRETT J. ROBERTS, & MELODEE A. WALKER

The Fluency Factor
Authentic Instruction and Assessment for Reading Success
in the Common Core Classroom
TIMOTHY RASINSKI & JAMES K. NAGELDINGER

Helping English Learners to Write—Meeting Common Core Standards, Grades 6–12
CAROL BOOTH OLSON, ROBIN C. SCARCELLA, & TINA MATUCHNIAK

Reading Across Multiple Texts in the Common Core Classroom, K–5
JANICE A. DOLE, BRADY E. DONALDSON, & REBECCA S. DONALDSON

Reading, Thinking, and Writing About History
Teaching Argument Writing to Diverse Learners in the Common Core Classroom, Grades 6–12
CHAUNCEY MONTE-SANO, SUSAN DE LA PAZ, & MARK FELTON

Engaging Students in Disciplinary Literacy, K–6
Reading, Writing, and Teaching Tools for the Classroom
CYNTHIA H. BROCK, VIRGINIA J. GOATLEY, TAFFY E. RAPHAEL,
ELISABETH TROST-SHAHATA, & CATHERINE M. WEBER

All About Words
Increasing Vocabulary in the Common Core Classroom, PreK–2
SUSAN B. NEUMAN & TANYA WRIGHT

PROFESSIONAL LEARNING IN ACTION

AN INQUIRY APPROACH FOR TEACHERS OF LITERACY

Victoria J. Risko / MaryEllen Vogt

Foreword by Douglas Fisher

TEACHERS COLLEGE PRESS

TEACHERS COLLEGE | COLUMBIA UNIVERSITY
NEW YORK AND LONDON

Published by Teachers College Press, 1234 Amsterdam Avenue, New York, NY 10027

Copyright © 2016 by Teachers College, Columbia University

Cover illustration inspired by Keith Vogt

Library of Congress Cataloging-in-Publication Data is available at loc.gov

ISBN 978-0-8077-5702-4 (paper)
ISBN 978-0-8077-7501-1 (ebook)

Printed on acid-free paper
Manufactured in the United States of America

23 22 21 20 19 18 17 16   8 7 6 5 4 3 2 1

*We dedicate this book to those colleagues
who have been our collaborators—
those who have shared in our journey by asking the difficult questions,
who have offered insights that challenged our thinking,
and who, in the process, have stimulated our own inquiry
and professional learning.*

Contents

Foreword

This book, *Professional Learning in Action: An Inquiry Approach for Teachers of Literacy,* will help close the "knowing/doing" gap. We have all experienced this gap. Simply said, most of us know more about teaching and learning than we actually implement in the classroom. For some teachers, the gap is wide. For others it's much smaller. Importantly, this does not mean that teachers with smaller gaps are more effective. It may be that they don't know as much yet, so the gap is small. Or it may be that they know a lot and work conscientiously to implement their expanding knowledge base. Also consider the teachers with wider gaps between knowing and doing. Some of these teachers know a lot but don't use that knowledge. There are all kinds of reasons for this gap. But, again, we all have a gap in knowing versus doing.

There are any numbers of reasons why good ideas are not implemented in classrooms, which is unfortunate given the amount of time and money that is put into helping teachers acquire the knowledge and skills necessary to do their jobs well. That's where *Professional Learning in Action: An Inquiry Approach for Teachers of Literacy* comes in. Vicki and MaryEllen provide a framework for supporting teachers in closing the knowing-and-doing gap. It's not just a set of random ideas that make this book so compelling. Instead, they have developed a systematic way to ensure that teachers are members of collaborative learning groups that harness the power of collective teacher efficacy. There is a significant and deep research base that supports collective teacher efficacy as one of the most powerful ways to positively impact student achievement.

One way to consider if something is worth implementing is to consider the impact that it can be expected to have on students' learning. A statistic that we can use to determine this is an effect size, which is really a numeric value that indicates the magnitude of the change that can be expected. Effect sizes also allow us to determine relative impact as well. For example, something with an effect size of .3 is less likely to improve students' learning than something with an effect size of .6 or .9.

Let's consider an example. John Hattie (2009) has been aggregating research and producing effect size information for educators to use. Teaching test-taking skills has an effect size of .27. Compare that with small-group instruction, which has an effect size of .49 and reciprocal teaching, which has an effect size of .75. Given limited time in the classroom, it seems wise to focus efforts on small-group instruction and reciprocal teaching, rather than teaching test-taking skills. But how many of us have been told by well-meaning leaders that we have to "get students ready for the tests"?

The effect size conversations can help focus discussion about what works and what should be implemented. Hattie noted that 95% of what teachers do, works when no growth over the course of the year is expected. In other words, most things we all do will impact students' learning, but not enough for them to gain a full year of learning for a year in school. Hattie determined that it takes an effect size of .40 or more to ensure that students get a year of learning for a year in school.

But this book, and this Foreword, are not about *what* should be implemented, but *how*. And that's where the effect size research makes a powerful point. The effect size for collective teacher efficacy is a whopping 1.57! Getting teachers together and supporting their collaborative thinking really works to improve student learning. If you are a leader of a grade level, department, or school, and you want to spend your time wisely, it seems more than reasonable to suggest that you invest heavily in collective teacher efficacy. If you are a teacher with a deep desire to ensure that your students learn, one of the most effective things that you can do is get together with your colleagues and collaborate on lesson design, strategy implementation, and analysis of student work. Unfortunately, most of us don't know how to do this. We are not sure what to talk about during these meetings, and often the conversation drifts to low-level logistics, rather than how to move the proverbial needle of student learning. Thankfully, *Professional Learning in Action: An Inquiry Approach for Teachers of Literacy* provides the tools needed to take teams from ideas to implementation.

—Douglas Fisher, San Diego, CA

Preface

When we were invited to write this book for the Common Core State Standards in Literacy Series, we anticipated writing a volume that would discuss how to help teachers, through professional development, become more comfortable and effective when teaching their students the literacy skills and strategies as outlined in the Common Core State Standards (2010). However, since we began working on this book, there have been some changes in the educational landscape, regarding both Common Core and professional development, that have influenced our thinking and writing. Among them are:

1. While the majority of states have adopted the Common Core State Standards (at the time of this writing), others have either adapted ELA Standards for their own needs, or they have dropped the CCSS altogether;
2. For states that are not using the CCSS per se, the English Language Arts Standards that have been adapted or developed are similar and of equal rigor;
3. While there are few research findings that show traditional professional development offerings positively impacting student learning outcomes (Yoon, Duncan, Lee, Scarloss, & Shapley, 2007), school districts continue to require and support these offerings with the expectation that they will enable teachers to plan lessons effectively based on the Common Core and/or other rigorous standards;
4. A few researchers and writers are suggesting that we move away from traditional *professional development* (PD) that is "done to" teachers and administrators. In contrast, they (and we) suggest that *professional learning* is a more relevant term, because it engages educators and other stakeholders in generating questions collaboratively that lead to investigation of problems

related to teaching plans, instructional decisions, and student achievement.

We mention these points because what we started writing didn't end up being what we finished writing. Although we started writing a book on professional development and the Common Core, our reading, research, and long discussions led us instead to propose a new approach to professional learning (not PD) that has, at its core, collaboration and inquiry. We posit that today's rigorous academic standards, such as the Common Core and Next Generation Science Standards, require more and higher levels of engagement in determining how to best prepare and support teachers and administrators for enabling all students to succeed. This type of engagement comes as a result of collaboration among all stakeholders, and through assessment of the needs and strengths of both students and teachers alike. Inquiry-based professional learning is predicated on determining the questions that need to be asked and answered in order to identify the problems that need to be solved.

Throughout this book, we provide a look into the collaborative, inquiry-based approach to professional learning undertaken by the fictional Blue Falls School District. The district happens to be in a state that has adopted the Common Core State Standards. However, if you are not using these particular standards, simply substitute whatever variations of the Common Core or other rigorous standards that you are using. When we use the term *standards*, we are referring to those that are used in your district.

In addition, it is beyond the scope of this book to provide specific examples and recommendations for professional learning that focus on subject area standards beyond the English language arts. However, the principles of collaborative inquiry, and the related implementation recommendations in this book, are certainly relevant and can be adapted easily for professional learning efforts in all disciplines. In essence, this book is intended for anyone who is involved in planning and implementing professional learning opportunities at the school and/or district level, and for courses that prepare educators for this work. Because the text emphasizes the importance of collaboration and inquiry by teams of educators, it is relevant for teachers, specialists, literacy and instructional coaches, curriculum leaders, parent representatives, administrators, and university educators. We have included examples of literacy teams collaborating at the Pre-K–2 level, as well as at the upper elementary, middle school, and high school levels.

ORGANIZATION OF THE TEXT

Each chapter has this organizing pattern:

- An opening graphic organizer explaining the chapter's structure;
- Realistic and detailed vignettes about literacy teams from the fictional Blue Falls School District, and their collaborative inquiry into an aspect of working with the Common Core ELA Standards;
- A focus on principles of inquiry-based professional learning that are Dynamic, Intense, Situated, Substantive, Collaborative, and Personal;
- An overview of the relevant research and theoretical constructs for the chapter's content;
- School-based examples, forms, charts, and graphs;
- Concrete connections between professional learning and rigorous standards; and
- Questions for reflection and discussion.

A brief explanation of each of the six chapters follows:

Chapter 1: Realizing the Power of Professional Learning. This chapter sets the foundation for our view of educators taking responsibility for their own learning through problem-solving actions that are deliberate and responsive to authentic problems. We discuss policies that affect professional learning, misconceptions that can inhibit such learning, and principles that guide an inquiry approach to professional learning.

Chapter 2: Supporting Teachers as Adult Learners. In this chapter we discuss the differences between how children and adults learn, with a brief review of adult learning theory and research. We suggest that collaborative, inquiry-based professional learning is differentiated, and is congruent with the research on how adults— teachers in particular—learn best.

Chapter 3: Using Assessment to Situate Professional Learning. The focus of this chapter is two-pronged: 1) assessing students' literacy strengths and needs, using a variety of methods and multiple indicators; and 2) assessing teachers' strengths and needs as related to literacy instruction. Data from these needs assessments lead to the collaborative generation of questions and identification of potential problems that may need to be investigated.

Chapter 4: Creating the Professional Learning Plan and Putting It into Action. In this chapter we discuss strategic actions for goal setting and implementing a plan for professional learning. We then present two methods—book study and lesson demonstrations—that foster inquiry, deepen professional learning, and examine applications of new ideas in practice.

Chapter 5: Sustaining the Professional Learning Plan. Additional methods that foster learning and systematic problem solving are presented in this chapter. Teacher research groups, family literacy study groups, lesson study, and peer and literacy coach mentoring are methods that engage analytical thinking and deepen understandings of how to apply new knowledge for optimal instruction and student learning.

Chapter 6: Evaluating and Understanding Change. In this final chapter we bring the collaborative inquiry process full circle, as we discuss a variety of authentic ways to assess the success of the professional learning efforts. We include an examination of the questions and problems that are identified during the inquiry process, as related to both student and teacher needs and strengths. Assessing the impact of professional learning efforts on student achievement and teacher change is also discussed.

We appreciate the suggestions of our anonymous reviewers— your supportive comments strengthened the book and let us know that we were headed in the right direction. We also thank Keith D. Vogt for his assistance and creativity in designing the figures that are found throughout the book. To Jean Ward and our editorial staff at Teachers College Press, we offer our appreciation for shepherding the book through to fruition. In addition, we're grateful to Dr. Susan B. Neuman and Dr. D. Ray Reutzel, Editors of the Common Core State Standards in Literacy Series, for their support of our work. Finally, we thank our families for their unwavering support of our academic interests and pursuits.

Our hope is that you will find this book intellectually challenging and motivating. You will see in the first chapter that this is not just another how-to book on professional development. Instead, right up front, we issue a challenge to you and your colleagues—to become a community of learners whose primary interest is improving instruction in order to enable all students to become fully literate. During the collaborative inquiry process that you will be undertaking with your fellow educators, we hope that you will reach new levels of understanding, expertise, and confidence about teaching literacy.

—vjr and mev

PROFESSIONAL LEARNING IN ACTION

AN INQUIRY APPROACH FOR TEACHERS OF LITERACY

CHAPTER 1

Realizing the Power of Professional Learning

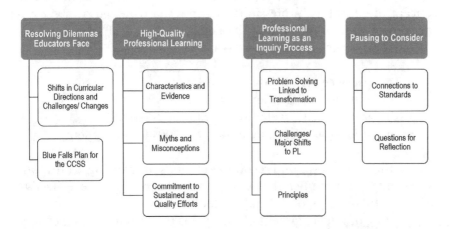

Professional learning engages our problem-solving abilities, and, in the process, prepares us to be thoughtful and deliberate in our response to both exciting and challenging events that accompany societal, educational, and policy changes. Included among these changes are increased diversity of students' cultural and linguistic histories; increased economic inequality and numbers of children living in poverty; increased attention to student dropout rates and literacy difficulties; policies advancing new standards; and educational innovations, especially within digital learning platforms. Being thoughtful and deliberate in our decision-making requires a shift in how our professional learning occurs, moving away from being told what to do as educators and moving toward taking agency for directing our own professional learning. *Our aim for the professional learning described in the chapters that follow is the enhancement of teachers' and administrators' abilities to address and resolve dilemmas they face when responding to multiple*

changes that impact teaching and learning. Professional learning occurs in the midst of engagement with authentic problems, in examining possibilities and different perspectives, and in implementing practices that will resolve those problems.

This view of educators taking responsibility for their own professional learning by engaging in problem solving is guided by a social constructivist view and transformational learning theory. The emphasis for learning moves away from a focus on what a person knows to how a person knows it (Rohlwing & Spelman, 2014). Interactive factors such as learners' motivation, cognition, emotion, affect, and attitude impact the success of professional learning opportunities. The concept of educators' professional learning has evolved over six decades through identifiable stages. Kragler, Martin, and Sylvester have labeled these stages (2014, pp. 484–495):

- the inservice era (1950s–1960s);
- the staff development era (1970s–1980s);
- the professional development era (1990s–2000s);
- the professional learning era (mid-2000s to the present).

And in this century we find recommendations for creating professional learning communities that engage in collaborative and collective inquiry (DuFour, DuFour, & Eaker, 2008).

Guiding our development of this text is the firm belief that changes and professional growth occur when we are directing our own learning and when that learning is situated within an examination of the realities we face. We choose to use the term *professional learning* instead of *professional development*, to reference the multiple opportunities that engage our thinking and our informed decision-making, and that advance our knowledge and expertise.

HOW ARE POLICY CHANGES AFFECTING PROFESSIONAL LEARNING EARLY IN THE 21ST CENTURY?

Perhaps the most comprehensive policy change affecting professionals is the recent state adoptions of either the English Language Arts Standards of the Common Core State Standards or another form of standards-based literacy education. As standards-based literacy education is brought to the forefront, we draw attention to its association

with the multiple challenges to teaching and learning that we described above (e.g., increased diversity of students' cultural and linguistic histories). Shifts in curricula and instruction that come with
implementing new standards can serve as a springboard for addressing
additional issues and challenges embedded in the school setting.

The English Language Arts (ELA) Standards of the Common
Core, for example, provide both anchor and grade-level standards for
Reading, Writing, Speaking and Listening, and Language (see Figure
1.1 [pp. 4–6] for a list of ELA anchor standards and their compo-
nents) and require major shifts in instruction (National Governors
Association Center for Best Practices & Council of the Chief State
School Officers, 2010). These standards identify what students need
to know when they graduate from high school in preparation for future education and careers. Shifts in instruction, particularly in grades
K–5, accompany the ELA standards, as illustrated in Figure 1.2 (p. 7).
The Common Core and other forms of standards-based teaching hold
promise of new directions for meaningful instructional and learning environments. Yet their implementation requires school districts'
commitment to high-quality professional development that will support teachers' remodeling of literacy instruction in ways that enhance
their own teaching and their students' learning, *and* respond to expected shifts in instruction (National Center for Literacy Education
[NCLE], 2014).

A commitment to high quality and effectiveness of educators at
all levels is a central feature of the Every Student Succeeds Act (ESSA,
2015). And consistent with the national movement to implement rigorous ELA standards, the ESSA focuses on improving resources to
low-performing schools and providing assessments and effective instruction that foster deeper learning of academic content.

CHALLENGES ASSOCIATED WITH IMPLEMENTING
THE COMMON CORE ENGLISH LANGUAGE ARTS STANDARDS

The National Center for Literacy Education (NCLE), representing a
coalition of 30 professional associations, educational policy organi-
zations, and foundations, completed a national survey of educators
across grade levels, subject matter, content areas, and roles, to examine their preparedness for the Common Core State Standards and
goals for learning experiences of students. As you read the results of

Figure 1.1. College and Career Readiness Anchor Standards for Reading, Writing, Language, and Speaking and Listening (K–5, 6–12)

College and Career Readiness Anchor Standards for Reading

Key Ideas and Details

1. Read closely to determine what the text says explicitly and to make logical inferences from it; cite specific textual evidence when writing or speaking to support conclusions drawn from the text.
2. Determine central ideas or themes of a text and analyze their development; summarize the key supporting details and ideas.
3. Analyze how and why individuals, events, and ideas develop and interact over the course of a text.

Craft and Structure

4. Interpret words and phrases as they are used in a text, including determining technical, connotative, and figurative meanings, and analyze how specific word choices shape meaning or tone.
5. Analyze the structure of texts, including how specific sentences, paragraphs, and larger portions of the text (e.g., a section, chapter, scene, or stanza) relate to each other and the whole.
6. Assess how point of view or purpose shapes the content and style of a text.

Integration of Knowledge and Ideas

7. Integrate and evaluate content presented in diverse media and formats, including visually and quantitatively, as well as in words.
8. Delineate and evaluate the argument and specific claims in a text, including the validity of the reasoning as well as the relevance and sufficiency of the evidence.
9. Analyze how two or more texts address similar themes or topics in order to build knowledge or to compare the approaches the authors take.

Range of Reading and Level of Text Complexity

10. Read and comprehend complex literary and informational texts independently and proficiently.

College and Career Readiness Anchor Standards for Writing

Text Types and Purposes

1. Write arguments to support claims in an analysis of substantive topics or texts, using valid reasoning and relevant and sufficient evidence.

Figure 1.1. (continued)

2. Write informative/explanatory texts to examine and convey complex ideas and information clearly and accurately through the effective selection, organization, and analysis of content.
3. Write narratives to develop real or imagined experiences or events using effective techniques, well-chosen details, and well-structured event sequences.

Production and Distribution of Writing

4. Produce clear and coherent writing in which the development, organization, and style are appropriate to task, purpose, and audience.
5. Develop and strengthen writing as needed by planning, revising, editing, rewriting, or trying a new approach.
6. Use technology, including the Internet, to produce and publish writing and to interact and collaborate with others.

Research to Build and Present Knowledge

7. Conduct short as well as more sustained research projects based on focused questions, demonstrating understanding of the subject under investigation.
8. Gather relevant information from multiple print and digital sources, assess the credibility and accuracy of each source, and integrate the information while avoiding plagiarism.
9. Draw evidence from literary or informational texts to support analysis, reflection, and research.

Range of Writing

10. Write routinely over extended time frames (time for research, reflection, and revision) and shorter time frames (a single sitting or a day or two) for a range of tasks, purposes, and audiences.

College and Career Readiness Anchor Standards for Language

Conventions of Standard English

1. Demonstrate command of the conventions of standard English grammar and usage when writing or speaking.
2. Demonstrate command of the conventions of standard English capitalization, punctuation, and spelling when writing.

Knowledge of Language

3. Apply knowledge of language to understand how language functions in different contexts, to make effective choices for meaning or style, and to comprehend more fully when reading or listening.

Figure 1.1. College and Career Readiness Anchor Standards for Reading, Writing, Language, and Speaking and Listening (K–5, 6–12) (continued)

Vocabulary Acquisition and Use

4. Determine or clarify the meaning of unknown and multiple-meaning words and phrases by using context clues, analyzing meaningful word parts, and consulting general and specialized reference materials, as appropriate.

5. Demonstrate understanding of figurative language, word relationships, and nuances in word meanings.

6. Acquire and use accurately a range of general academic and domain-specific words and phrases sufficient for reading, writing, speaking, and listening at the college and career readiness level; demonstrate independence in gathering vocabulary knowledge when encountering an unknown term important to comprehension or expression.

College and Career Readiness Anchor Standards for Speaking and Listening

Comprehension and Collaboration

1. Prepare for and participate effectively in a range of conversations and collaborations with diverse partners, building on others' ideas and expressing their own clearly and persuasively.

2. Integrate and evaluate information presented in diverse media and formats, including visually, quantitatively, and orally.

3. Evaluate a speaker's point of view, reasoning, and use of evidence and rhetoric.

Presentation of Knowledge and Ideas

4. Present information, findings, and supporting evidence such that listeners can follow the line of reasoning and the organization, development, and style are appropriate to task, purpose, and audience.

5. Make strategic use of digital media and visual displays of data to express information and enhance understanding of presentations.

6. Adapt speech to a variety of contexts and communicative tasks, demonstrating command of formal English when indicated or appropriate.

Source: National Governors Association Center for Best Practices & Council of Chief State School Officers. (2010). *Standards of the Common Core State Standards (English Language Arts)*, www.corestandards.org

Figure 1.2. Instructional Shifts Expected with Implementation of CCSS

1. Balance of Text Genre
2. Increase of Text Complexity
3. Students Generating Evidence-Based Responses
4. Writing from (and Integrating) Multiple Sources
5. Writing in Multiple Genres (e.g., arguments, explanatory papers, narratives)
6. Building Academic Vocabulary

Source: Adapted from National Governors Association Center for Best Practices & Council of Chief State School Officers. (2010). *Key Shifts in the English Language Arts, Common Core State Standards* www.corestandards.org

this study, think about how you would answer the question on your preparation to implement the Common Core or other new forms of standards. Would your responses be similar to those reported on the NCLE survey?

Data from the 2013–2014 survey of 3000, reported in Figure 1.3 (p. 8), indicated that the majority of teachers felt that their schools' literacy curriculum materials were not well aligned with the new standards. Also, teachers felt unprepared to implement the new literacy state standards and believed that there were problems associated with lack of time for intense and prolonged professional development and insufficient mechanisms to promote the collaborative work needed for change. NCLE concluded that "the transition to the new standards seems to be going best when teachers are highly engaged in the process and have time to work together to use their professional expertise to bring all students to higher levels of literacy" (NCLE Report, 2014, p. 11).

We provide the NCLE example to illustrate a change in curricular direction that is having a profound impact on teaching and learning in some school districts. Next we introduce you to the educators at Blue Falls School District, who are facing this curricular change and initiating their own program of professional learning. Then we discuss features of high-quality professional learning with evidence supporting these features, and common misconceptions that can intrude on positive outcomes. Next we discuss more specifically the role of inquiry, major shifts that an inquiry approach requires of professional learning, and guiding principles. We conclude this chapter by drawing connections between the features of high-quality

Figure 1.3. Summary of NCLE 2013–2014 Findings

1. Nationwide, most teachers do not yet feel well prepared to implement the new literacy standards, especially with high-needs students.
2. Teachers report that working with other educators is the most powerful form of preparation.
3. Unfortunately, the amount of time teachers have to work together is brief and shrinking, and most teachers are not substantially involved in planning how their schools will implement the new literacy standards.
4. Where teachers are significantly involved in renovating literacy instruction, positive changes are well under way.
5. Purposeful professional work that draws on the talents of everyone in the system is strongly associated with progress in standards implementation.
6. Teachers in all disciplines are actively engaged in shifting literacy practices, and those who have the opportunity to work together are making the biggest shifts.
7. When given the opportunity, teachers are owning the change by innovating and designing appropriate lessons and materials.

Source: National Center for Literacy Education (NCLE), 2014. *Remodeling literacy learning together. Paths to standards implementation.*

professional learning and challenges associated with implementing the Common Core State Standards. Also, we provide discussion questions that we hope will encourage you to pause and consider how the content of this chapter relates to your teaching and professional learning.

CONNECTIONS TO INSTRUCTION: INTRODUCTION TO THE BLUE FALLS VIGNETTE

The Blue Falls School District provides an example of how one district is preparing to initiate its professional learning program. In this vignette we describe professional learning efforts around the Common Core, which was adopted by their state, but the implementation challenges as described are relevant to any district's adoption of new, rigorous standards. Here and in the chapters that follow, Blue Falls' situation and actions will serve as an anchor for our discussion of the professional learning concept and methods for achieving its goals.

One School District's Preparation for Professional Learning

Demographics and history. In July, Dr. Rosa Sanchez, Superintendent, Blue Falls School District, is collaborating with her instructional leadership team and a representative group of classroom teachers to plan for a second year of a multiyear professional development project. Blue Falls County Schools are located in a Southeastern urban school district that serves approximately 90,000 students, grades Pre-K–12. Fifty-six percent of the students receive free or reduced-priced lunch. The ethnic composition of the students is African American (46%), White (34%), Hispanic (16%), and Asian (4%). Twenty percent of the District's students are English learners, and 100 language groups are represented in the student population.

For two prior years, the instructional leadership team and classroom teachers focused their professional learning efforts on meeting STEM (i.e., science, technology, engineering, and math) goals. For their changes and impact, they received commendations from the state department of education and national leaders for strong programs, steady increases in student achievement in the STEM areas, and increases in high school graduation rates. Blue Falls is also known in the state as one of the few countywide school districts that has maintained a community outreach program for at least two decades, with parent participation in school programs and student service community projects.

Current planning for English Language Arts. Following the focused work on STEM goals, Dr. Sanchez and her colleagues turned their attention to literacy goals and increased alignment of instruction with the English Language Arts Standards of the Common Core State Standards (CCSS). The CCSS were adopted by the state and the school district during the previous academic year. For at least two decades, Blue Falls has implemented a Balanced Literacy curriculum with guided reading instruction in small groups and shared reading and writing activities in large and small groups, in the elementary and middle grades, and integrated language arts in the high school. Their guided reading program is organized around a literature anthology program adopted by the school district.

A need for change in professional learning efforts. Overall, professional learning methods for literacy instruction and alignment with the CCSS have lacked specific content focus, coherence across professional development sessions, and teacher involvement in planning and changes. Annual professional development efforts varied from after-school study groups to full-day meetings with guest speakers during the summer months. Reading specialists in the elementary and middle school grades work with students who are experiencing difficulties and serve as coaches to mentor teachers. Teachers' evaluations of the earlier professional development efforts were mixed, with some teachers benefiting and others reporting a need for additional support.

Dr. Sanchez and her team of instructional leaders (i.e., principals, curriculum specialists, and reading specialists) and classroom teachers are initiating a new program of professional learning that will respond to the strengths of the district and the needs of the teachers and students during the transition to implementing fully the CCSS. They have already decided on two features that will characterize their work. First, they will find blocks of time for teachers and administrators to work together—this is their first priority—so that they can initiate a problem-solving process for identifying and responding to challenges they face. Second, they will develop and implement a comprehensive needs assessment with data collected from all members of the educational staff, students, and families. These data will inform their early plans for their professional learning work. As the plan develops, they will identify specific needs and include those (including administrators, teachers, specialists, and outside experts) who are knowledgeable on particular topics to provide guidance for problem solving.

The following questions are offered to invite your reflections on Blue Falls' initial professional learning efforts. These questions will be addressed in the remainder of the chapter.

1. What are possible strengths and limitations of the professional learning program that is in the planning stage?
2. How can team planning that includes both administrators and classroom teachers impact a school-wide implementation plan?
3. How will experts who are both outside and within the school district become part of the team to guide professional learning?

HIGH-QUALITY PROFESSIONAL LEARNING AS A PROCESS

There is little doubt that high-quality professional learning opportunities are required to support teachers' progress in understanding what is expected with new waves of standards-based instruction. Learning how best to apply these understandings to their own practices will enhance their students' learning and performance. Before you read the following section, in which we identify evidence-based characteristics of professional learning programs, pause to identify elements that have been most helpful for your professional learning. Identify, also, those characteristics that have been painful and less than helpful. How do these align with what researchers have identified?

What Have We Learned from Decades of Research?

From a wide body of research, there is a consensus that highly successful professional learning associated with changes in teacher practices and increased student achievement has the following characteristics:

- Educators at all levels within school districts (i.e., administrators, specialists, coaches, and classroom teachers) can benefit from professional learning activities. While the long-term goal is to effect optimal classroom instruction, administrators and specialists must be prepared to support teachers' efforts and goal setting.
- Intensive, ongoing, and long-term professional learning that is connected to teachers' classroom contexts and practices is most likely to impact students' achievement gains (Darling-Hammond, Wei, Andree, Richardson, & Orphanos, 2009), with greater gains associated with long-term and sustained professional learning (Banilower, 2002).
- Multiple and carefully planned applications of newly acquired knowledge to instruction, coupled with guidance, instructional demonstrations and models, and teacher reflection, should be embedded in the work of the classroom teachers and evaluated frequently for impact (Desimone, Porter, Garet, Yoon, & Birman, 2002).
- Professional learning that attends to students' literacy difficulties is more likely to be successful when there is an alignment between instructional goals and specific attention to the school's resources, curriculum, assessment and accountability practices, and school-wide initiatives (Garet, Porter, Desimone, Birman, & Yoon, 2001).
- Professional learning must address academic content and pedagogical knowledge that relates to the concepts and skills teachers want their students to learn, with particular attention to those areas that are troublesome for their students (Blank, de las Alas, & Smith, 2007).

- Strong collaborative relationships among teachers, with teacher involvement in decision-making for professional learning goals and content, are associated with higher teacher involvement and, in turn, with higher student achievement (Darling-Hammond et al., 2009).
- Structural supports facilitate professional learning; these include allocation of sufficient time for meeting goals and varied organizational arrangements for bringing educators together for planning and evaluation (Darling-Hammond et al., 2009).
- Successful professional learning opportunities are responsive to the needs of the school personnel, implementing differentiated mentoring and professional activities to address teachers' experience (e.g., beginning vs. more experienced teacher histories) and needs (Carroll & Foster, 2010).

What Are Some of the Myths and Misconceptions of Research That Can Inhibit Robust Professional Learning?

Running counter to implementing highly effective professional learning programs are multiple myths, faulty expectations, and misunderstandings of research findings; these can inhibit the success of even the best professional learning efforts. As you read the following misconceptions that we have identified, reflect on your own context and the educators with whom you work.

Misconception 1. Professional learning programs have a history of affording student achievement gains. Instead, there are tremendous challenges to impacting student performance and gains (Yoon et al., 2007). Of more than 1,300 studies on professional development, only nine that met What Works Clearinghouse standards for rigor reported student gains.

Misconception 2. Early indicators, as judged by student achievement test scores, can determine whether the professional learning program in place is headed in the right direction; low scores indicate a need to discontinue professional development as planned and start again in setting goals and an implementation plan. This advice is counterproductive and typically cuts short the long-term investment that is needed for positive impact. Continuous evaluation must take place so that appropriate and timely changes to the plan occur. If there are unintended outcomes, for example, students' scores may go down initially (due to changes in instruction or texts or content) before growth and change result in a positive trajectory; multiple measures of student learning can identify areas requiring further accommodations (Guskey, 2014a).

Misconception 3. Teacher satisfaction with one-day workshops can be a catalyst for long-term change in teacher performance. There is no evidence to support this supposition. Ball and Cohen (1999) argued that these programs typically are "intellectually superficial, disconnected from deep issues and curriculum and learning, fragmented, and cumulative" (pp. 3–4). Conversely, students' gains are associated with an average of 49 hours of intensive professional development work (Yoon et al., 2007).

Misconception 4. Teachers prefer that experts outside of their school district conduct their professional learning. Research indicates that having both outsiders and insiders provides for a balance of perspectives and expertise for facilitating professional learning. Teachers surveyed preferred learning opportunities led by peers or leaders of their own school district and found these opportunities relevant to their specific needs and situated within the problems they were experiencing (Yamagata-Lynch & Haudenschild, 2008).

Misconception 5. There is a strong association between increased teacher knowledge and positive changes in student performance. While this assertion is accurate in many instances, teacher knowledge will not have a positive impact on student learning unless it is coupled with changes in instruction with appropriate adjustments for the students involved. Increasing teacher knowledge is complex and often difficult to achieve in ways that student performance changes significantly, unless students and situational factors are also addressed simultaneously (Desimone & Stucky, 2014).

What Are the Big Takeaway Ideas?

Professional learning is not a taken-for-granted activity that can be implemented quickly or easily. To be impactful, professional learning should be a robust endeavor, with ongoing activity engaging all levels of school personnel, families, and relevant community members. Now, let's turn to professional learning as an inquiry process.

PROFESSIONAL LEARNING AS AN INQUIRY PROCESS

In their analysis of *How People Learn* (1999), Bransford, Brown, and Cocking argue that active inquiry that engages problem solving is the catalyst linking learning and change. And, of course, professional learning activities are organized to sustain the learning of both teachers and students, and change conditions that are inhibiting this learning. Darling-Hammond, known for her leadership and research on professional learning, also emphasizes the importance of problem solving for knowledge acquisition and for making changes in instructional practices.

> Great teachers and people who learn effectively obviously understand content in ways that allow them to draw out the big ideas, the core concepts, the fundamental relationships in a field of study, and use those understandings in productive ways to do things, to solve problems, to produce ideas, and so on, so that the people can use their knowledge. (Umphrey, 2009, interview with Darling-Hammond, p. 19)

There is evidence that inquiry as a process for engaging professional learning around shared problems and dilemmas is powerful across teacher groups, regardless of years of experience. For example, Windschitl, Thompson, and Braaten (2011) describe high levels of change among beginning teachers when they adopt a "problematized view" of teaching and learning and participate in collaborative inquiry for problem resolution. Problem solving engages professionals in "learning through their practice" (Lieberman & Miller, 2014).

When problem solving is the catalyst for professional learning, teachers analyze real-classroom and instructional dilemmas, and the resulting analytical thinking fosters *active learning and doing* within authentic contexts while *responding* to challenges and *transforming* teaching practices. In Figure 1.4, we illustrate the synergistic relationships across problem solving, learning and doing, and responding and transforming. These relationships are formed when inquiry guides professional learning.

Figure 1.4. Professional Learning as an Inquiry Process

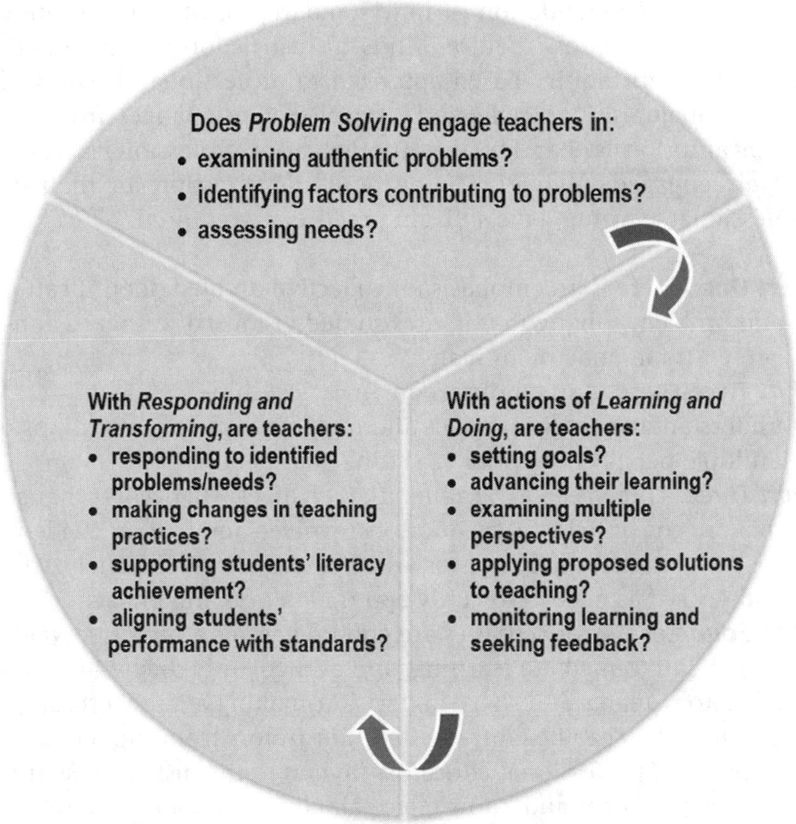

Does *Problem Solving* engage teachers in:
- examining authentic problems?
- identifying factors contributing to problems?
- assessing needs?

With *Responding and Transforming*, are teachers:
- responding to identified problems/needs?
- making changes in teaching practices?
- supporting students' literacy achievement?
- aligning students' performance with standards?

With actions of *Learning and Doing*, are teachers:
- setting goals?
- advancing their learning?
- examining multiple perspectives?
- applying proposed solutions to teaching?
- monitoring learning and seeking feedback?

Specific questions can then be assigned to the areas identified on the sections in Figure 1.4, to guide the work and teacher actions, and to reflect on if and how teachers are involved in the robust process of professional learning. These questions are organized around three sets of actions: Problem Solving, Learning and Doing, and Responding and Transforming. For the action of Problem Solving, the emphasis is on identification and analysis of problems and a needs assessment. For Learning and Doing, educators are involved in goal setting, advancing learning and applications of information for problem solving, and monitoring their own learning. Responding and Transforming focuses on an analysis of changes and on aligning changes with goals.

MAJOR SHIFTS IN APPROACH TO PROFESSIONAL LEARNING

Just as the implementation of new standards, such as the Common Core State Standards, requires shifts in instruction (as identified in Figure 1.2), an inquiry-based approach to professional learning also requires major shifts. Professional development changes from what is typical to forms that actualize the power of professionals who are actively engaged in generating purpose and direction for their own professional learning. Five shifts in practice are required.

Shift One: There is an emphasis on collective problem identification and problem solving that invites shared visions, and shared and agreed-upon enactment plans.

Shift Two: There is an emphasis on analytical thinking, deep understandings of local issues and problems, and examinations of multiple perspectives prior to setting goals.

Shift Three: There is an expectation that changes will occur—changes that are generated by the educators involved and that are evidence-based—and that once changes are in place they will be analyzed and revised as needed to verify appropriateness and impact.

Shift Four: Leaders of activities are chosen based on their knowledge and ability to mediate learning, and as mediators they will join the educators' teams and share in decision-making and goal setting. These leaders can be educators/administrators from the school district *and* professional educators invited to the district to share their experiences and knowledge gained from exploring similar problems in other settings.

Shift Five: Increasingly, professional learning efforts are situated in teachers' own classrooms, with attention to their individual pedagogical strengths and needs. This shift to embedded or situated learning requires differentiation of professional learning efforts. Methods for differentiating are described in Chapters 4 and 5.

PRINCIPLES OF AN INQUIRY MODEL OF PROFESSIONAL LEARNING

Highly effective professional learning opportunities are *dynamic, intense, situated, substantive, collaborative,* and *personal.* From empirical research and descriptions of highly effective professional learning programs (Desimone & Stuckey, 2014; Garet et al., 2001), we derived principles that work in tandem to engage inquiry and affect professional learning. For impact and sustainability, the collective applications of these principles will more likely have a positive effect on teacher learning, and in turn, teacher learning is associated with instructional changes that result in student learning.

Professional learning is dynamic. This principle is integral to all others because it signals the expectation that professional learning will be active, enabling of different perspectives, and developed within a climate that promotes trust and agency among the participants. Histories and identities of administrators, specialists, coaches, teachers, and families are respected as educators engage in dialogue to set goals for addressing challenges (Fullan & Knight, 2011). When trusting relations and peer networks are formed among school personnel (Byrk, Sebring, Allensworth, Luppescu, & Easton, 2010), it is more likely that plans are sustained.

Rather than being directed solely to classroom teachers, the inquiry model of professional learning acknowledges the role administrators play in fostering a climate of trust and collective responsibility for teachers' learning (Desimone, 2002). Teacher capabilities are part of a collective enterprise (Newmann, King, & Youngs, 2000). Taking time to build a climate of trust fosters teachers' willingness to share their challenges and practices, and invite feedback and suggestions from their peers (Hord & Tobia, 2012). In turn, teacher buy-in increases when teachers take responsibility for their own learning (Sailors & Price, 2010).

Professional learning is intense, with a particular emphasis on problem solving. The principle of intensity includes prolonged engagement, duration, and a deliberate focus on problem solving. Teachers who are engaged in prolonged and sustained goal-oriented work (with at least 14 hours of professional learning, with an average of 49 hours associated with highly effective programs) are more likely to increase student achievement (Yoon et al., 2007). With this investment of time in professional learning, Yoon and his colleagues concluded that students' achievement can be boosted by as much as 21 percentile points.

Districts that commit to duration of professional learning (Garet et al., 2001) typically have multiple organizational formats for teacher engagement (e.g., team meetings, video demonstrations, quick reads, online work) and dedicated time for teacher mentoring. Mentoring, in the forms of modeling, observing, co-planning, and coaching, is associated with higher student gains (Elish-Piper & L'Allier, 2010). If teachers are not supported in the application of newly learned knowledge, there is little likelihood that students will benefit from teachers' professional learning (Yoon et al, 2007).

Professional learning is situated. Embedded in real-world teaching events and challenges, professional learning provides a way to bridge relationships among theory, research, and practice in classrooms (Fisher & Frey, 2013). In a collective study of their own problems, teachers learn from each other, test and apply their ideas in their classrooms, evaluate changes and gains, and receive mentoring and feedback (Desimone & Stuckey, 2014).

Professional learning is substantive. To achieve the substantive principle, professional learning focuses on teachers' acquisition of knowledge at a deep level, facilitates goal setting and implementation/ evaluation plans, and is guided by research-based strategies for adult learning. Teacher learning of academic and pedagogical content and how students learn academic content are associated with changes in teacher knowledge and student achievement (Yoon et al., 2007). And when content and pedagogical knowledge are coupled, it is more likely that teachers will be able to apply their knowledge to their teaching practices (Neuman & Cunningham, 2009).

For professional learning to be substantive, content and goals must be compatible with each other and coherent with the school's curriculum, state standards, and school initiatives that are familiar to the teachers (Penuel, Gallagher, & Moorthy, 2011). Required, too, are evaluations that include multiple and continuous assessments that address all aspects of the goals in place—goals for enhanced teacher knowledge and skills, improved classroom instruction, and student achievement. Multiple forms of data (including observations and interviews) inform the recursive process of goal setting and changes in professional development work (McDonald, 2001). It is difficult, if not impossible, to associate professional learning with teacher and student changes with a poorly designed evaluation system (Yoon et al., 2007.

Professional learning is collaborative. This principle builds on the notion that a community approach can affect the whole school, promoting school-wide change that goes beyond but includes individual change. Professional learning is successful when there are ample opportunities for collegial inquiry, support, and feedback (Dagen &

Bean, 2014), in a school climate where teachers feel ownership of their learning (Newmann et al., 2000). There is appreciation and respect for teachers' discretion and collective problem-solving capabilities. Professional learning also occurs when groups make progress in achieving particular goals. For example, grade-level teachers may be an appropriate team to pursue lesson development in particular content areas (Garet et al., 2001), whereas teams with members across grades and content areas may be needed to direct lesson development for cross-curricular teaching.

Professional learning is personal. Even when professional learning efforts are evaluated as successful for their positive impact on student achievement, teacher involvement, satisfaction, and change vary across teachers. There is great variability in teacher performance and satisfaction, even within programs that are identified as successful for their positive impact on student achievement (Carroll & Foster, 2010). Thus, it is important to have differentiated support for professional learning, accounting for teachers' questions, problems, histories, and prior knowledge/experience. Adjusting professional development offerings and forms of support is associated with higher levels of scaffolding, especially when these supports are designed to address teachers' particular and individual needs (Santagata, 2009).

Taken together, these principles are the vital elements that sustain professional learning efforts, and when they are in place they provide the structure for organizing the learning and problem-solving opportunities that require decision-making, deep learning of issues, and putting strategies in place to resolve these issues.

CONNECTIONS TO THE COMMON CORE STATE STANDARDS AND OTHER STANDARDS-BASED POLICIES

In a June 3, 2014 survey of the School Superintendents Association by the Alliance for Excellent Education (Amos, 2014), more than half of the state superintendents and school administrators indicated that they had invested at least two years in implementing the Common Core State Standards. Others (approximately 7%) planned to begin the process of implementing these standards the following year, 2014–2015. These school leaders were optimistic about the direction and requirements of the standards, supporting the opportunity for advancing the learning of their students, but they expressed concerns about a lack of instructional materials aligned with the standards and insufficient time for professional development. They feared that changes occasioned by the new standards were happening too quickly, without sufficient time to "get it right." These concerns are similar to those expressed by the teachers surveyed by the NCLE (2014), who indicated that their curriculum was not aligned with the Common Core, and they felt less than prepared for the changes required of them.

In our example of the Blue Falls School District, Dr. Sanchez and her colleagues are not hurrying the process of change. They understand the challenges that accompany shifts to a new set of standards and expected shifts in instruction. They are making a long-term commitment to preparing teachers to teach the English Language Arts Standards of the Common Core and have several foundational steps in place—team building across different levels of educators within the school district and with parents and the community; planning for data collection to identify needs, concerns, and visions; and organizing teams and time for meaningful inquiry, planning, and goal setting.

Questions for Reflection

1. Examine your own professional learning history to identify characteristics that you viewed as helpful for your professional learning and those that made it difficult. What implications do you draw from those experiences?

2. Interview a teacher, an administrator, and a school parent to learn their views about professional learning sessions being scheduled during the school year. Some of these sessions occur during school time, reducing the time each week for instruction of students. Do they think this is time well spent? Why or why not? If yes, what specific outcomes can they identify? If not, what would they recommend as an alternate activity? How do their viewpoints relate to our six principles of professional learning?

3. Choose one principle and do some additional reading of related research and/or examples of how it is applied to practice. What did you learn? What would you share with your administrators, reading specialists, and other teachers and parents?

CHAPTER 2

Supporting Teachers as Adult Learners

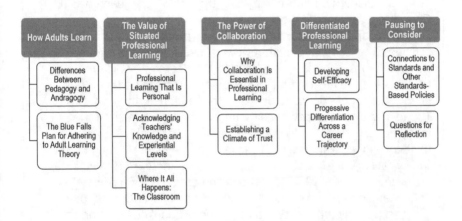

In this chapter we begin with a discussion of adult learners, as distinguished from children and adolescents. We reinforce the professional learning principles of *situated, collaborative, dynamic,* and *personal,* while attending to the unique needs, preferences, and goals of adult learners. We then describe self-efficacy, which can be both a goal and an outcome of inquiry-based professional learning. We also suggest that differentiated professional learning for teachers can lead to greater transfer of new information learned, and application and retention of more effective instructional methods. We conclude the chapter with questions for discussion and reflection.

The Blue Falls leadership team has decided to engage in collaborative inquiry for the upcoming professional learning related to the implementation of the Common Core ELA Standards. The first topic in their investigation is to review research on how adults learn.

Connections to Instruction:
Continuing the Vignette

One of the important realizations that the Blue Falls instructional leadership team experienced during the previous professional development efforts on meeting STEM requirements was that the district's teachers are a very diverse group, in their teaching experience, content knowledge, pedagogical skills, and attitudes about learning new information and instructional techniques. Given this insight, the team became committed to better meeting the needs and honoring the strengths of district teachers during the upcoming professional learning efforts targeting the English Language Arts (ELA) Common Core State Standards.

In preparation for developing the new professional learning activities, the leadership team reviewed data from the previous STEM PD evaluations, especially as related to the degree to which the teachers felt the professional development activities had met their needs. These data provided direction to the team in three ways: 1) The teachers were nearly unanimous in their appreciation of the many opportunities the STEM PD gave them to collaborate with their colleagues. This aspect of the PD had the highest rating on the survey; 2) For some teachers, the activities during the STEM PD were irrelevant to their teaching questions and contexts. Unfortunately, this understanding came too late in the PD cycle. Information about what teachers perceived they needed had been overlooked; 3) Although the STEM PD evaluations were completed anonymously, it was evident, after the fact, that some teachers' lack of success with the STEM PD may have been predicted by determining teachers' needs prior to the beginning of the STEM professional learning efforts.

As the leadership team began planning for the professional learning focusing on the ELA Common Core Standards, they decided to take an inquiry stance while investigating the following:

- What research says about how adults learn
- What research says about the effect of collaboration on adult learning, since this appeared to be a strength of the previous PD effort
- What research says about what motivates adult learners to apply new information and approaches in their individual context

To focus their study, the team leaders determined the following guiding questions:

- How can we, as instructional leaders, best support teachers as learners?
- How do we build upon the collaborative spirit of the teachers that was generated previously in order to develop a climate of trust for subsequent professional learning?
- Is it possible to differentiate professional learning to meet teachers' needs and strengths, while attending to their individual teaching questions and contexts?

DO CHILDREN AND ADULTS LEARN DIFFERENTLY?

For years, educational researchers have debated the following conflicting suppositions:

- Learning is essentially the same for all people, whether they are children or adults.
- Learning is not the same for children and adults, and there are identifiable differences in how each group learns.

While investigating these suppositions, researchers of adult learners in the 1970s were unable to identify a single theory or set of principles that clearly defines adult learning (Rohlwing & Spelman, 2014). To ameliorate this dilemma, Malcolm Knowles (1984) introduced to the United States a term and concept that had been used by adult educators in Europe for more than a century. In contrast to *pedagogy* (the art and science of teaching), Knowles suggested using the term *andragogy* (*andra* = manly), which describes instruction for adult learners. For many years, his principles of andragogy guided the field of adult education in the development of instruction and materials (Atherton, 2013). As you read about each of Knowles's principles think about the ways in which they apply to you as a learner. In what ways are they relevant for the teachers with whom you work?

1. Adults (those 18 and over) need to know a purpose for learning something new.
2. Adults' experiences, even with mistakes, provide a basis for their subsequent learning.
3. Adults, when learning something new, want to be responsible for their own decisions as they progress toward independence.

4. Adults most want to learn that which is immediately relevant to their own situations.
5. Adults respond better to internal motivation than to outside motivators.
6. Adult learning is more problem-centered than content-oriented.

As we think about planning effective professional learning for teachers, we suggest framing Knowles's principles for adult learners as follows:

1. Teachers need to know how learning a new concept or instructional method will impact their particular students.
2. Teachers' instructional knowledge and experience should serve as a foundation for new pedagogical learning.
3. Teachers want to make their own decisions as they learn and apply new instructional methods and approaches, and this can be facilitated during professional learning.
4. Teachers most want to learn that which they can apply immediately in their own classrooms with their own students.
5. Teachers respond best to that which leads to positive changes in their students.
6. Teachers will gain deeper understandings of instructional applications that address their questions within inquiry-based, dynamic approaches to professional learning than they will from traditional, "sage-on-the-stage" professional development sessions.

Keeping these points in mind, consider four recurring themes in adult learning that have emerged from the research literature: Experience, Reflection, Dialogue, and Context (Rohlwing & Spelman, 2014, pp. 233–235). As you look at each theme in Figure 2.1 (pp. 26–27), read the description and then consider the implications that we formulated. Do the implications of each theme match or differ from those of your particular context (school, district, or university)? If so, in what ways are they the same or different?

In the next section, we talk briefly about embedded, situated learning, and why it is so much more relevant to teachers than the ubiquitous "sit-down-and-listen" inservices.

WHAT IS EMBEDDED OR SITUATED LEARNING?

Note in Figure 2.1 that the fourth recurring theme in research on adult learners is *context*. As indicated previously, teachers are more likely to value professional learning that is relevant, personal, and directly applicable to problems they are facing and questions they are asking about students in their own classrooms. Some refer to this as *embedded* learning. In this book, we call it *situated* learning because this type of adult learning experience is collaboratively planned by teachers and other educators, such as administrators, support personnel, and other stakeholders. Most important for teachers is that the professional learning is personal, situated within their own classrooms, with their own students, questions, problems, and issues. Situated learning isn't unique to educators; in many professions, on-the-job training is the norm, both for initial and follow-up preparation. Think about the how the following learners master the skills of their professions:

- Doctors, nurses, and dentists
- Chefs
- Professional football players
- Concert pianists
- Orchestra conductors
- Plumbers
- Architects

Can you imagine people in any of these careers learning only by listening and watching, and not by doing? Similarly, in effective teacher education programs, prospective teachers observe teachers and apply what they've learned by teaching real students in real classrooms throughout their preparation. However, once they're on the job, many professional learning opportunities revert to having teachers just sitting and listening, in settings far removed from their own students.

In contrast, embedded professional learning is situated in teachers' classrooms, and it is responsive to what teachers want and need. This professional learning is characterized by

- making explicit teachers' questions and problems;
- immediate practice and application of newly learned information and teaching techniques;
- experiential learning that occurs throughout the school day;

Figure 2.1. Recurring Themes in Adult Education Research

Theme	Description of Theme	Implications for Professional Learning
Experience	• Experience can be both a positive and negative influence for adult learners.	• When planning professional learning for a group of teachers, determine the amount and type of experience that the teachers have related to the topic.
	• Some experiences enable the learner to make connections that assist in learning new information.	• As with students, teachers benefit from making connections to past learning and experiences. Help them understand the positive and negative influences of their experiences, and how these might impact their understanding of and response to the topic at hand.
	• Other experiences can negatively impact the learner by becoming a barrier to new learning.	• Some teachers believe that because they know and have experience with a topic, it is unnecessary for them to delve further into it. This is more likely to be a problem if a teacher's association is negative: "I tried that activity before and it didn't work."
	• For adult learners, more experience is not always better; instead, the quality of the experience is the more important factor.	• Teachers, regardless of whether previous experiences with instructional methods or techniques have been positive or negative, benefit from identifying and articulating questions for problems they want to solve or issues they want to resolve. This process is at the heart of inquiry-based learning.
	• Adults learn from their experiences in different and varied ways.	• What resonates for one teacher may be off-putting to another. Try to know as much as possible about the teachers for whom you are planning professional learning.

Reflection	• One of the most important differences between learners who are adults and those who are children is the ability to reflect on what is being learned. • For adult learners, reflection is a critical component of the learning process.	• Throughout this book, you are asked to reflect on points that are made and, as part of that reflection, to relate them to your own situation or context. • Providing adequate time for reflection during professional learning activities is critically important. • The reflective periods may be private: "Think for a moment about ___ and what it might look like in your own classroom." • Or the reflective periods may be public ("Take a moment and share a time when ___ happened in your own classroom. Explain to a partner how you ___." • What's important is that you remember to plan for breaks throughout workshop or during a post-observation conference, for teachers to actively reflect on their practice.
Dialogue	• Meaningfully engaging in dialogue with colleagues develops collegiality and a common language. • Dialogue is an integral part of transformational learning as "people construct and deconstruct assumptions with others" (Rohlwing & Spelman, p. 235).	• Reflection and dialogue go hand-in-hand. Following a period of reflection, ask teachers to engage in a structured dialogue (e.g., with prepared discussion questions or conversation prompts).
Context	• Adult learners benefit from learning experiences that are situated in their own context.	• If your educational background and experience are in the secondary grades, you're probably not eager to attend a workshop in a kindergarten classroom. • Or if you're a kindergarten specialist, AP classes at the high school aren't particularly relevant to your work. Teachers relate best to what they know.

- concrete connections made between past and current learning;
- active, sustained engagement;
- self-reflection and analysis of practice;
- variety according to teachers' needs, interests, and learning styles (e.g., book study groups; lesson study; analysis of lesson videos; journaling);
- transfer of new learning to address problems and apply to teaching practices;
- attention to adult learning theory; and
- an atmosphere of sharing, collegiality, interaction, and collaboration.

Throughout this book, to illustrate the principles of situated professional learning, we will provide specific suggestions so that teachers find professional learning relevant, meaningful, and appropriate for their own classrooms.

WHY IS COLLABORATION ESSENTIAL FOR ADULT LEARNERS?

Teachers know from research and experience that learning is a social process for children and adolescents, and they regularly include in lessons meaningful, collaborative activities that encourage students to interact with others. Part of helping students learn how to work collaboratively and cooperatively is creating a climate of trust in the classroom, where students learn how to share ideas, agree and disagree with others in a respectful manner, praise good ideas, and participate equitably.

Developing a climate of trust and nurturing effective skills of collaboration during professional learning are of equal importance for adults. When learners—of all ages—are interacting and collaborating during a structured discussion or a problem-solving task, they are practicing social skills while applying the concepts and specialized language of the content they are learning (see Figure 2.2 for types of collaborative groups).

Perhaps you are involved in a school-wide Professional Learning Community (PLC). Within this collaborative group, educators assume an inquiry stance for problem solving, usually around a specific topic or issue. All members of the PLC have equal status, and collaboration is a given, as is a climate of trust. Everyone can speak freely, assured that all ideas will be considered openly and fairly. Developing shared

Figure 2.2. Types of Collaborative Groups

Type of Collaborative Group	Description	Examples
Within School	Teachers in grade-alike or content-alike groups	Lesson-planning groups; study groups or book groups
Across School	Mixed grades and subject areas; can include any combination of teachers, administrators, paraprofessionals, staff, and parents	PLCs (Professional Learning Communities); initiative implementation (e.g., RTI [Response to Intervention] or SIOP [the Sheltered Instruction Observation Protocol] model)
Within District	Grade-level teams from various schools; subject area teams from various schools; grouped teams: Pre-K, primary, intermediate, middles school, high school	Curriculum development; textbook adoption committee; professional learning activities
Across Districts	Cross-curricular groups; across grade-level groups	Conferences; professional learning activities
Within Community	School/university groups	Lab schools: preservice teachers, inservice teachers, and professors jointly conduct and disseminate research
Across Community	All stakeholders (churches, service groups, library/media, etc.)	Promote and implement educational initiatives

understandings of problems and generating collaborative solutions is the goal of the PLC, as well as any associated professional learning.

At this point you might be thinking, "In your dreams . . . you don't know *my* school!" Obviously, a well-functioning PLC or any other type of collaborative group doesn't happen overnight. Tenets of cooperative learning suggest that teachers keep students together in the same cooperative learning groups for at least 6 weeks, because it generally takes this long for groups to gel and develop *interdependence*. This happens when the climate of trust is so well established that the need to depend on others for accomplishing goals is internalized. For adults and younger students alike, it takes time to develop trust and confidence in the ideas of others. The time span needed to establish a group's interdependence may vary considerably, depending on a variety of factors, such as the frequency, quality, relevance, and sustainability of professional learning offerings. However, once a climate of trust is established, the collaborative results of professional learning can be significant. Recall that the Blue Falls leadership team established an effective climate of collaboration with their previous professional learning efforts. With their new project, they will be able to develop this further, with the goal of group member interdependence and a climate of trust.

WHAT IS SELF-EFFICACY?

When you were a child, did someone read to you the classic book *The Little Engine That Could*? Watty Piper, the author, was a pseudonym for Arnold Munk, who was a partner in Platt & Munk, the first publishers of the book in 1930. As you may recall, the little blue engine was asked to pull a long train up and then down a big mountain, and when the pulling became very difficult, the engine repeated, "I think I can. I think I can." Once he made it over the top of the mountain, on the trip down, the little blue engine repeated simply, "I thought I could. I thought I could." The little blue engine exemplifies self-efficacy in action!

Efficacy might be described as "the power to produce an anticipated outcome." A successful experience leads to self-efficacy, and when an outcome from a task is positive, efficacy is increased. As an example, when a teacher tries a new technique several times, and an outcome such as student performance improves with each attempt, the teacher's self-efficacy related to using the technique is likely to increase.

Teachers who possess self-efficacy share a number of characteristics (Reeves, 2011; Tschannen-Moran & Chen, 2014; Zepeda, 2012). Self-efficacious teachers

- hold personal convictions about what they can accomplish;
- use research to inform their use of instructional techniques;
- take on challenging tasks that they believe they can do;
- stay focused on accomplishing what they set out to do;
- exert effort on endeavors they believe will result in positive outcomes;

- believe they can complete tasks and reach goals;
- marshal their energy and resources to manage problems;
- believe their actions are the primary influence on the academic success of their students; and
- celebrate their students' academic successes.

In sum, efficacious teachers are those who get things done because they believe they can.

However, in our present educational climate, we often create roadblocks that hinder teachers' development of self-efficacy. For example, many schools have a myriad of initiatives that teachers are asked to implement, often at the same time. Therefore, it's not surprising that when asked to attend *another* workshop on one of the school's initiatives, some teachers balk, complain, or don't show up. Reeves (2011) has coined the term *initiative fatigue* to describe how competing initiatives and the resulting lack of focus undermine teachers' and administrators' energy, leading to exhausted, emotionally spent educators.

Mandated initiatives, by school and/or district decision-makers, have been shown to lessen teachers' self-efficacy. In contrast, when teachers have a locus of control over initiatives they believe will benefit their students academically, they feel more efficacious. Not surprisingly, teachers who are deemed efficacious are more likely to have students who perform at higher academic levels when compared to students whose teachers demonstrate low efficacy (Reeves, 2011). For successful, efficacious teachers, a cycle of reinforcing behaviors develops and then fortifies their feelings of self-efficacy (see Figure 2.3).

As you look at this cycle, you might think, "Yes, but that's not really what happens every time a teacher tries something new in the classroom!" And you're absolutely right. Sometimes, something intervenes that breaks the cycle. Tshannen-Moran and McMaster (2009) suggest that once the self-efficacy cycle is attained, it is quite stable until there is a "jarring experience [that] provokes a reassessment" (p. 239). What follows is a classroom example that illustrates this point.

Sarah is an 8th-grade math teacher in a middle school in which 32% of the students are English learners. She has been going through professional learning with SIOP, an empirically validated instructional model for English learners and other students that focuses on teaching content concepts and academic language concurrently and

Figure 2.3. Self-Reinforcing Cycle of Efficacy

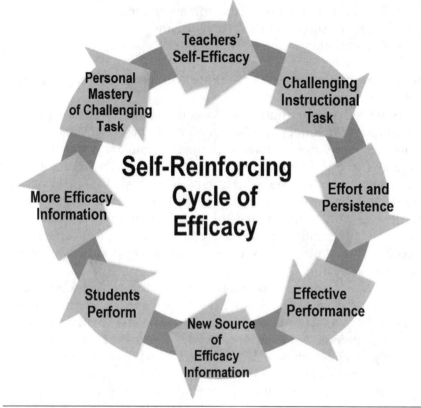

Source: Adapted from Tschannen-Moran & McMaster, 2009.

systematically (Echevarria, Vogt, & Short, 2017; Vogt, 2012). Sarah is currently working on Interaction, one of the eight SIOP components, and she is beginning to implement in her classroom the first two features of this component:

- frequent opportunities for interaction and discussion between teacher and student, and among students, which encourage elaborated responses about lesson concepts;
- grouping configurations that support the content and language objectives of the lesson.

Whereas Sarah has had considerable success in her heterogeneous classroom with the first three SIOP components, and she's feeling energized and confident about her ability to eventually implement the model well, when she begins working on the first feature in the Interaction component (frequent opportunities for interaction and discussion), she becomes discouraged and disillusioned. While her native English-speaking students readily talk with each other about group work they're doing, for the most part the English learners in her class hardly speak at all. They have little difficulty with their math assignments, but as soon as Sarah asks them to engage in an instructional conversation, using the academic vocabulary she has pre-taught and modeled, her English learners sit passively and in silence.

The first time this happened in Sarah's class, shortly after she had put her students in groups of four or five, she had no idea what to do, even though she is usually confident about how to handle nearly any situation in her classroom. When it happened again over the next few days, she knew she had to seek help to find out how to develop her English learners' oral language proficiency so they could participate more fully in math discussions. Sarah's difficulty with this particular problem caused her efficacy to waver.

What happened to Sarah was not only a "jarring experience"; it also represents an *implementation dip in self-efficacy*, which researchers have reported happens as teachers begin to implement an initiative that involves changing what they have been doing (Tshannen-Moran & McMaster, 2009, p. 232). So what did Sarah do to help increase the oral engagement of her English learners? Fortunately, she had an effective SIOP coach who was able to build upon the SIOP professional learning sessions she had attended. Over the next week, Sarah and her coach did the following:

1. Sarah invited her coach into her classroom to observe three math lessons so he could better understand the teacher's concern about English learners not participating orally in class.
2. Her coach then modeled how to create and use meaningful, authentic sentence frames that provided a scaffold for students who were reluctant to speak. Some of Sarah's native English-speaking students also benefited from temporary use of the language frames that served as scaffolding.
3. Sarah and her coach discussed how to meaningfully group and regroup students to maximize English learners' and other students' oral participation.

4. Sarah's coach shared an article about how to chunk information during teaching to break up oral presentations, thus providing more time for students to engage in meaningful talk and collaborative group work.

Sarah's coach may have been familiar with Tschannen-Moran and McMaster's (2009) study of varied formats for professional development. The researchers discovered that the format that included coaching and support while teachers were developing a new teaching skill was related to increased implementation and self-efficacy as measured by efficacy scales.

So, here's the point: All teachers occasionally have experiences in the classroom that rattle their confidence. These experiences, if increasingly frequent, can so adversely erode a teacher's confidence that his or her self-efficacy deteriorates. Understanding how to help adult learners through the process of developing and rebuilding efficacy is a critical element of effective professional learning. And to do this, those who are involved in professional learning activities need to know about the teachers with whom they are working.

WHAT IS DIFFERENTIATED PROFESSIONAL LEARNING?

The teachers and administrators who attend any professional learning offering obviously have varied motivations and interests for doing so. These most likely depend on the participants' knowledge, experience, and feelings about the particular topic, as well as the credibility, relevance, and liveliness of the presenter. Reflect on an inservice you attended where you found the topic uninteresting, irrelevant, and boring. Perhaps the presenter's style was that of the "sage on a stage," and there was little interaction among participants. How engaged were you? How eager were you to try the ideas that were presented?

Now consider how you would have felt if the inservice had been tailored to your specific questions, needs, interests, and learning style. What would have been your feelings in the days leading up to the workshop if you knew beforehand that it was being designed, in part, to meet your needs?

There have been a number of studies conducted over the past 35 years that have clearly demonstrated that grouping students for the majority of their instructional day by ability is deleterious and inequitable, primarily because of the poor quality of the instruction provided for low-achieving students (Callahan, 2005; Hiebert, 1983; Lucas, 1999; Oakes, 1985; Vogt, 1989). Therefore, teachers have been encouraged to differentiate instruction, rather than keep students in designated ability groups for long periods of time.

Like students, teachers may also benefit from professional learning that is differentiated for their particular abilities, interests, and needs. Although this practice is not currently widespread, several experts in professional learning have suggested that attending to teachers' background knowledge and experience when planning professional learning is an important consideration (Fisher & Frey, 2014; Glickman, Gordon, & Ross-Gordon, 2013). In such professional learning, teachers provide information about their interests, strengths, and areas in which they feel they need more information. They also determine their personal learning goals for professional learning activities, are provided with hands-on and self-directed activities for their diverse learning styles, and are encouraged to relate what they're learning to specific students in their own classrooms (see Chapters 4 and 5 for specific information about hands-on and self-directed activities that can be chosen by teachers to meet their teaching and learning goals).

As an example of how teacher education and professional learning can be better tailored to meet teachers' needs and strengths, the National Academy of Education (NAEd) convened a panel of 10 literacy scholars to determine what teachers need to know and be able to do to be effective teachers of reading. The Reading Subcommittee, of which MaryEllen Vogt was a member, approached their task by focusing on what teachers of reading need to know and be able to do *at particular points in their career*. These points were labeled as *preservice, apprentice, novice, experienced*, and *master* teacher (Snow, Griffin & Burns, 2005, p. 6) (see Figure 2.4).

Along these points, which are fluid rather than static, teachers develop types of knowledge, or "ways of knowing," that were identified by Snow et al. (2005) and colleagues as follows:

- *Declarative Knowledge:* A *Preservice* teacher is acquiring knowledge from books, lectures, and observations about child psychology and development, instructional approaches, and curriculum, generally in undergraduate education (or in 5th-year teacher education classes). Preservice teachers, especially

Figure 2.4. Points on a Teacher's Career Trajectory

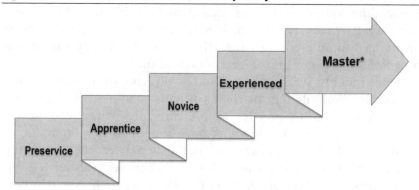

*In reality, these points on the trajectory are not equally spaced. It may take a relatively short time for a teacher in the "Apprentice" phase to move to "Novice," while it might take several years for an "Experienced" teacher to become a "Master" teacher.

Source: Adapted from Snow, Griffin & Burns, 2005, p. 6.

those without classroom experience, have mostly Declarative Knowledge, with very little of the other types of knowledge at this point.

- **Situated, Can-Do Procedural Knowledge:** An *Apprentice* teacher (a student teacher or 1st-year teacher) has ample declarative knowledge, and can probably can handle common classroom routines and situations (e.g., reading aloud to a small group of children, or teaching a phonics lesson to children who are not struggling with reading). Other types of knowledge are beginning to develop as more experience is attained.
- **Stable, Procedural Knowledge:** A *Novice* teacher (perhaps in the first 3years of teaching) has enough knowledge and experience to plan and carry out instruction under normal conditions or circumstances. This teacher still needs guidance and structured support to manage situations out of the norm.
- **Expert, Adaptive Knowledge:** The *Experienced* teacher can handle a variety of instructional challenges, can identify problems and seek out answers from research, and can take a leadership or consultant role with other teachers.
- **Reflective, Organized, Analyzed Knowledge:** The *Master* teacher has the experience and knowledge to provide professional learning, be a consultant, and collaborate with faculty in providing preservice teacher education.

Teacher education and professional learning within a developmental framework posits that teachers are more likely to grow in knowledge and experience when their current point on the teaching trajectory is acknowledged and nourished. Professional learning is differentiated and subject to analysis throughout a teacher's career. According to Snow et al. (2005) and colleagues, this is predicated on a presupposition of *progressive differentiation,* defined as "a process of development in which the capacities being used at any point are analyzed and elaborated, in response to evidence that they fall short" (p. 6).

In other words, if we use information about what a teacher knows about teaching reading at a particular point in her career development, we can use this information for tailoring her professional learning. This is in marked contrast to what we usually do—provide a one-size-fits-all program of professional development, not considering—or worse, disregarding—where a teacher might be on the career trajectory. When we ignore during professional learning what adults know about a topic, we are rejecting not only their experiences but also them as individuals (Zepeda, 2012).

The report of the NAEd Reading Subcommittee provides a road map for planning teacher education and professional learning based on teachers' career trajectories and their increasing knowledge and experience *over time.* It is beyond the scope of this text to go into further detail, but if you are responsible for providing professional learning in the teaching of reading, you are encouraged to read the committee's full report (Snow et al., 2005).

Other researchers have also suggested that planning differentiated professional learning is necessary if change in practice is the desired goal. Fisher and Frey (2014) state:

> Sometimes teachers have a deep knowledge of their content area, but not how to teach it. Other times, teachers have superior pedagogical skills, but not the level of expertise required by their disciplines. And still other times, teachers know their content well, understand and can implement general teaching approaches, but cannot teach their specific content (p. 205).

Fisher and Frey suggest that, just as with students in a classroom, the content, processes, and products of professional learning may need to be differentiated according to teachers' needs and strengths. To begin the process of differentiation for teacher development, it may be worthwhile to develop individual profiles that include information about each teacher's professional preparation, teaching experiences, and interests. Along with other assessed information, these profiles can then be used to inform the planning of professional learning activities. (See Chapter 3 for examples of teacher assessment instruments.)

CONNECTIONS TO PRINCIPLES
OF EFFECTIVE PROFESSIONAL LEARNING

In order for professional learning to resonate with adult learners, it needs to be **situated** in the context in which they will practice and master their new learning, whether that is a classroom, hospital, fire station, tennis court, or golf course. Within this context, adults can **personalize** and internalize new information and practices. Further, new learning experiences that are **dynamic** encourage adult learners to feel confident that they can, indeed, apply their new learning in practical and useful ways. Finally, professional learning that fosters **collaboration** among adult educators models the very processes that we encourage in classrooms, where interdependence and eventual independence are the goals.

CONNECTIONS TO THE COMMON CORE STATE STANDARDS
AND OTHER STANDARDS-BASED POLICIES

The Common Core State Standards for English Language Arts (National Governors Association Center for Best Practices & the Council of Chief State School Officers, 2010) require that teachers:

- know the essentials of teaching reading (Declarative Knowledge), and
- be intuitive, highly skilled, and able to teach all students to read complex texts deeply, thoughtfully, and with purpose (Stable, Procedural Knowledge; Expert, Adaptive Knowledge).

Is it reasonable to expect new teachers (apprentice level) and those in the first 3 years of teaching (novice level) to get equal benefit from identical professional learning activities as their more experienced peers? What would be the expected outcomes for each group? And might it not be more effective to look at the teaching demands of the Common Core and collaboratively plan differentiated professional learning according to where teachers are on the career trajectory?

Perhaps some of the Common Core topics are appropriate for one-size-fits-all activities (Declarative Knowledge). The following topics come to mind because they are well known and may require just a quick review:

- the purposes of the Common Core Standards;
- the purpose of the Anchor Standards;
- what the Common Core Standards are by grade level;
- how the Common Core Standards are organized; and
- what is meant by "vertical alignment" and "instructional shifts."

But other topics that require sophisticated teaching skills, such as how to teach close reading and how to identify and teach complex academic language, may need a differentiated type of professional learning for teachers at the novice and apprentice levels. And let's not forget that years of teaching do not always correspond to the quality of the teaching in a particular classroom. In Chapter 3 we discuss in detail how to create an assessment plan that captures teachers' interests, pedagogical knowledge, skills, and needs, in order to foster situated and appropriate professional learning.

Learning Forward Standards for Professional Learning. We have considered another set of standards for professional learning while writing this text. The *Learning Forward Standards for Professional Learning* (2011) are congruent with our approach to inquiry-based, collaborative professional learning. In a nutshell, the standards suggest that effective professional learning should include:

1. learning groups that focus on goal setting, shared responsibilities, and ongoing progress;
2. instructional leadership that is supportive and dedicated to developing educators' capabilities;
3. ample and appropriate resources for promoting professional learning;
4. the collection and analysis of a variety of sources of data for different purposes;

5. professional learning that is attentive to theory and research about how humans learn;

6. implementation that focuses on improvement of teacher efficiency and student achievement over time; and

7. results that are in line with student achievement, academic standards, and teacher performance. (For a thorough discussion of these standards, see Guskey, Roy, & von Frank, 2014.)

Questions for Reflection

1. Think about your own context for work (school, district, university). How do the principles that are essential for adult learning and are most relevant to this chapter pertain to you as an adult learner?

   - Situated
   - Collaborative
   - Personal

2. In what ways does self-efficacy about your work impact how you approach your job each day and the daily decisions that you make?

3. Go back to the opening of this chapter and review the statements about what adult learners need. Think about yourself as an adult learner.

   a. If you could plan your own professional learning, what would you include?

   b. What types of activities would you want to engage in?

   c. What would you never want to include?

   d. What do your answers to these questions tell you about what differentiated professional learning might look like for the particular teachers with whom you work?

Using Assessment to Situate Professional Learning

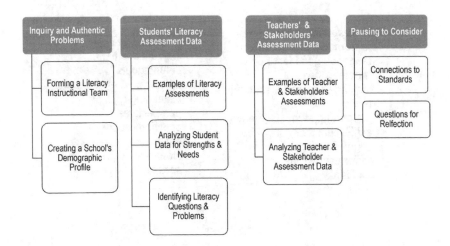

In this chapter we discuss the importance of situating needs assessments within an inquiry stance that invites problem identification from multiple perspectives. Multifaceted needs assessments invite feedback from school personnel, students, and parents; this results in a rich data set that engenders questions, identifies problems, and leads to potential changes needed to support student learning and teacher effectiveness. A careful analysis of the data should identify patterns of instructional needs, those of students and of teachers. Once problem areas are clearly identified, goals for professional learning can be determined. In this chapter we reinforce that professional learning should be *situated, personal, collaborative,* and *substantive*.

As depicted in Figure 3.1 (p. 42), several questions guide the needs assessment process within "Problem-Solving," and they provide a framework for the remainder of this chapter.

Figure 3.1. Professional Learning as an Inquiry Process

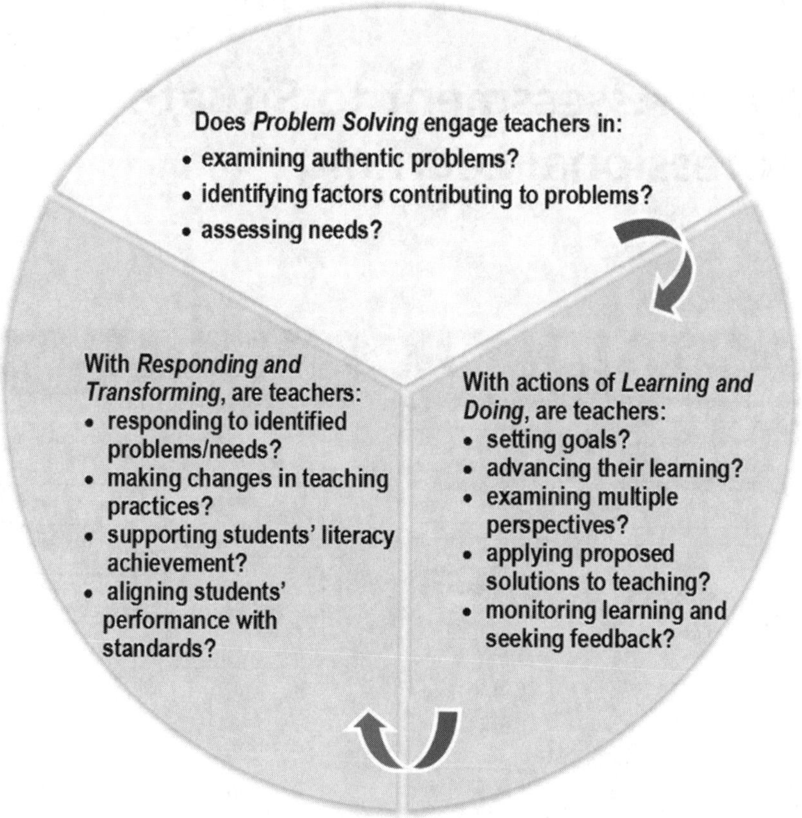

Does *Problem Solving* engage teachers in:
- examining authentic problems?
- identifying factors contributing to problems?
- assessing needs?

With *Responding and Transforming*, are teachers:
- responding to identified problems/needs?
- making changes in teaching practices?
- supporting students' literacy achievement?
- aligning students' performance with standards?

With actions of *Learning and Doing*, are teachers:
- setting goals?
- advancing their learning?
- examining multiple perspectives?
- applying proposed solutions to teaching?
- monitoring learning and seeking feedback?

Dr. Sanchez and the instructional leadership team from Blue Falls next turned their attention to planning a multifaceted needs assessment for students, teachers, and parents. Let's join them now as they begin this process.

Connections to Instruction: Continuing the Vignette

Rather than engaging in the typical practice of using current trends in literacy instruction to determine the content of professional learning sessions, the Blue Falls literacy team instead began the next phase of their collaborative inquiry by focusing on students' reading achievement in the district.

The following questions guided the team's inquiry:

- What do we need to know about our students' preparedness to meet the rigorous Common Core ELA Standards?
- What are students' strengths in reading, writing, listening, and speaking?
- What are students' weaknesses in reading, writing, listening, and speaking?
- How will we obtain and use student literacy achievement data?

Together the instructional team listed a variety of sources of information about students' literacy strengths and needs, including the following:

- student work samples from varied grade levels (such as writing samples);
- informal assessments of phonemic awareness, phonics, vocabulary knowledge, fluency, and comprehension;
- teachers' anecdotal reports about students' reading behaviors (such as knowledge of speech-to-print for very young children, and information from older students' reading logs);
- silent and oral reading assessments;
- benchmark assessments generated from the district program; and
- standardized achievement test results for reading and language arts.

Also, at one of their early meetings about student data, the district assessment analyst met with the team and explained how to interpret trend data coming from the district's standardized test results. He made suggestions for how they could draw some generalizations from both the informal and formal data they were collecting. Additionally, the assessment analyst offered to meet with the school teams as a group, to provide them with assistance in reviewing student achievement data. The team then set enhanced student learning across the district as their long-term goal for gathering and analyzing the student data.

To reach this goal, the team considered the second part of the needs assessment process, which required teachers' input from across the district. In preparation for creating a needs assessment of teacher knowledge and support for the new Common Core ELA Standards, the team reviewed what they had learned from their investigation up to this point:

- The importance of teachers' knowledge, skills, motivation, values, and concerns;
- The teachers' ability to identify and resolve problems; and
- The school and community's expectations for student learning.

These considerations led the team to realize that they shouldn't be the only ones gathering and analyzing student achievement data. Granted, it would be beneficial for Dr. Sanchez's instructional team members to have student achievement information available, but as soon as they provided schools with the data they had collected, the inquiry process for the individual educators in the schools would be compromised. In fact, upon receiving the data, the reactions of teachers and administrators in the schools might be something like, "Okay, tell us what we are doing wrong and what we are supposed to do about it." This was the antithesis of the spirit of collaborative inquiry that the instructional leadership team was trying to establish.

Upon this realization, the instructional leadership team's role shifted to data facilitators, whereby they would assist schools in gathering and analyzing their student achievement data. With the end goal of enhanced student learning in place, teachers and administrators from each school were provided the opportunity and support to collect and analyze their own student data, as well as draft a needs assessment for their school that would lead to question identification, goal setting, and ultimately a professional development plan. This work at the school site would be completed in tandem with the district's instructional leadership team.

Taking what they had learned from their research and discussions, each of the instructional leadership team members scheduled meetings with their own school's teachers and administrators. For the remainder of this chapter, as an example, we'll move to Blue Falls High School, and the work the faculty and staff did to: a) better understand their students' literacy strengths and needs; and b) articulate the questions they needed to ask in order to identify their school's literacy instructional issues and problems.

HOW DO WE ENGAGE TEACHERS
IN INQUIRY AND EXAMINATION OF AUTHENTIC PROBLEMS?

In Chapter 1 we learned that the teachers of the Blue Falls School District had completed their first year of implementing the new state standards that were based on the Common Core Standards. At the end of that year, Dr. Sanchez and her instructional leadership team realized that progress in aligning the curriculum with the standards required further work, because teachers were frustrated with what they viewed as a lack of support and a coherent plan for addressing these new standards. This problem is similar to ones reported by many teachers across the nation; they feel ill-prepared for teaching with standards that are requiring shifts in their instruction and curriculum (NCLE, 2014). For example, while many teachers have high levels of knowledge of guided reading instruction given their long history with a balanced literacy curriculum, these same teachers may not feel adequately prepared to teach and engage students in close readings of complex texts, as required by the ELA standards. Identifying and examining these authentic problems of both students and teachers is the purpose of the needs assessment process. But before problems can be identified, needs and strengths must be ascertained, and it takes a team to do the necessary investigating (see Figure 3.2).

Figure 3.2. Steps in Planning a Multifaceted Literacy Needs Assessment

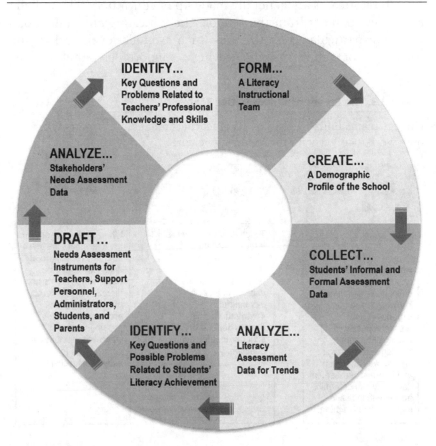

Forming a Literacy Instructional Team

There are multiple steps involved in conducting a needs assessment (Fisher & Frey, 2014; Vogt & Shearer, 2016; Sleezer, Russ-Eft, & Gupta, 2014). The first part of the process entails determining who is going to draft it. A school-based literacy instructional team best knows the students, teachers, and literacy issues in their school, and collaboratively, with the rest of their staff, they're able to establish a common vision for the school's literacy program. They work together to ask questions, identify needs, collect data, make data-driven decisions, support teachers with evidence-based practice, create short-term and long-term goals, and enhance their own and other teachers' efficacy related to literacy teaching. The value of having a **collaborative** literacy instructional team is in their collective knowledge and expertise, ownership of the process, and ultimately, we hope, empowerment (see Figure 3.3).

Literacy teams are generally made up of educators, staff, and, ideally, a few parents from the school. The educators and staff should represent particular constituencies, such as grade-level teachers; department- or subject-specific teachers; support personnel (reading

Figure 3.3. The Power of Collaborative Teams

Literacy teams utilize the strengths of teachers and administrators when they work together with the following beliefs:

Knowledge and Expertise	Ownership	Empowerment
Teachers are closest to their own teaching. They know what works and what doesn't. Given the opportunity to collectively use their knowledge and experience, and respected research findings in teaching reading and language arts, as well as formal and informal assessment data, they can determine how to enhance and improve their teaching.	Teachers want to feel as if they "own" their jobs. They consider themselves professionals, those capable of making meaningful contributions to the literacy goals of their schools, district, and community.	When, as a collaborative team, teachers are given authority for important decisions about the fundamental nature and direction of the literacy program, they are provided with possibilities for empowerment that are not available to individual teachers.

specialist; instructional coach; media specialist); special education teachers; and administrators. The teams can range in number from 7 to 15 members (depending on the size of the school)—not too many to hinder getting work done, but enough people to distribute responsibilities equitably. Learning how to function as an effective team may take a little time, especially if teachers in a particular school are used to working autonomously, and if the culture of the school doesn't foster administrators and teachers working together, and/or parent involvement in committees or teams. The following characteristics of highly effective instructional teams may be helpful to think about as the group is getting started (Vogt & Shearer, 2016):

- *Shared identity situated in the school:* "We're all in this together, and we have a common goal."
- *Clarity of the role of the instructional team:* "We understand what each of us needs to do to accomplish the goal, and I have a personal responsibility to complete particular tasks."
- *High level of collaboration among team members:* "We understand that we can get more accomplished together than we can individually."
- *Administrative support:* "We, as administrators, welcome the opportunity to work together with teachers and parents."
- *Effective decision-making strategies:* "We have a plan for agreeing and disagreeing respectfully with each other, so that we can make decisions and accomplish the goals we set."
- *Continuous self-assessment of tasks remaining and tasks completed:* "We are committed to monitoring what we are doing to ensure that we're making progress toward the goal."

Every task of the literacy instructional team has as its goal ensuring that all students in the school receive the most effective and appropriate literacy instruction possible. As the literacy team gets started with the task of creating a needs assessment, it is imperative to communicate openly the following information to all stakeholders:

- what the purpose of the team is, such as determining goals for the literacy program at the school;
- who will be involved in the process, including stakeholder groups in the school: students, teachers, administrators, and parents;

- who will be privy to the information gathered; and
- who will be involved in decision-making along the way.

Everyone in the school needs to understand that the literacy team doesn't hold the "power." While members of the team are the data collectors and information disseminators, all educators, students, and parent representatives, in collaborative fashion, will share the work of making decisions about the future direction of the literacy program.

Creating a Demographic Profile of the School

The next step in the needs assessment process is to create a demographic profile of the school. This is most likely readily available, perhaps on the school and/or district website. While everyone on the literacy instructional team may believe they know their own school's profile, there may be some surprises, such as the increasing number of English learners in the school during the past 3 years, or how many students receive free or reduced-price lunches. The following information is usually present in a school's demographic profile:

- student population (number of students at each grade level);
- socioeconomic level(s) represented;
- ethnicities of student population;
- stability of student population;
- percentage of English learners (at present and during the past 5 years);
- attendance rates;
- graduation rates (if high school);
- percentage of students with special needs receiving services; and
- professional demographics of teachers, administrators, and support personnel.

A note of caution is warranted when compiling demographic information. Be especially sensitive to how information is written and how language is used. This will be a public document and it should be read and edited, if necessary, by those representing the different constituencies on the literacy team.

HOW DO WE COLLECT STUDENTS'
INFORMAL AND FORMAL LITERACY ASSESSMENT DATA?

A comprehensive needs assessment provides information about the current status of a school's literacy (or other) program, and suggests benchmarks for its evaluation. Its purpose is to collaboratively identify existing problems through the examination of needs and strengths related to a particular topic or issue. The results of the needs assessment can be used to articulate problems, prioritize goals, determine plans to reach these goals, and apportion funds and resources. Most important, through systematic inquiry, a needs assessment ensures that *actual* rather than *perceived* problems are identified and addressed (Vogt & Shearer, 2016).

To accomplish this goal, a needs assessment investigates academic information about all students in the school, including those who are socioeconomically disadvantaged, gifted and talented, English learners, designated as having special needs, and so forth. An inherent danger in gathering academic information about particular subgroups is to overgeneralize the findings about each. As an example, some English learners are gifted and socioeconomically disadvantaged. Some special education students are English learners, and some socioeconomically disadvantaged students are gifted and talented . . . and so on. Therefore, caution is advised when gathering and analyzing academic information about a school's students and families. Take a look at achievement trends *over time* for subgroups, and then focus on the students as individuals, rather than as members of a particular subgroup.

Several organizational questions need to be answered by the school literacy instructional team at the beginning of the needs assessment process. These include:

1. What student performance data do we need to collect (informal, formal, standardized)?
2. Who will gather the student performance data and organize them for accessibility by all team members?
3. Who will summarize and report the student performance data?
4. To whom and in what format will the student performance data be reported?
5. What is the time frame for collecting the student performance data?

6. What is the time frame for summarizing and reporting the data?

7. How will the literacy team ensure the privacy of student data and accompanying reports?

Figure 3.4 includes examples of literacy assessments that would provide substantive information for creating a school's literacy achievement profile. Teachers will have some of this information in their classrooms; however, unless a climate of trust (see Chapter 2) has been established, some may be reluctant to share their students' literacy data. Teachers need to feel confident that academic needs assessment data will be used for the purpose of identifying *school-wide* questions, issues, and problems, and that this information will not be used for punitive purposes.

Once the assessment data are gathered, the literacy instructional team must organize them so that they can be analyzed thoroughly. Spreadsheets are helpful because data can be recorded by grade level and analyzed across grade levels. For example, an elementary

Figure 3.4. Examples of Data to Collect for Literacy Needs Assessment

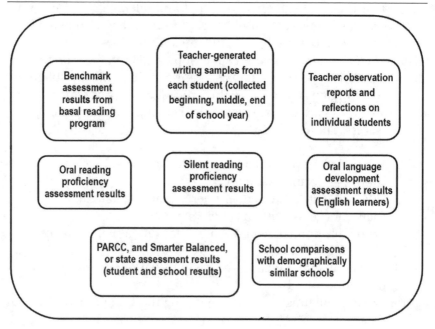

school may choose to look at data grade by grade, while the literacy instructional team at Blue Falls High School may decide to organize their data by departments (such as English, Math, Science, History). In whatever ways the data are organized, they must be easy to access so that questions can emerge and problems can be identified during analysis.

Analyzing Literacy Assessment Data for Trends

The next step in the needs assessment process is to analyze the student data that have been collected. Several of the guiding questions that the Blue Falls district instructional team used to guide their search may be appropriate to your school and district as well:

- What do we need to know about our students' preparedness to meet the rigorous state ELA standards?
- What are our students' strengths in reading, writing, listening, and speaking?
- What are our students' weaknesses in reading, writing, listening, and speaking?

One of the biggest challenges in analyzing current standardized literacy test data for trends over time, such as those from the Partnership for Assessment of Readiness for College and Careers (PARCC) and Smarter Balanced tests based on the Common Core State Standards, as well as other state tests, is that establishing trends is challenging whenever new academic standards are implemented. This is due to a number of factors, including:

1. Both the standards and the accompanying curriculum based on the standards have been implemented for a short period of time;
2. With standards based on the Common Core, there is a new way of testing students—no longer multiple-choice with bubble-in response sheets, but tests that are taken independently on a computer, with responses that mediate subsequent questions and tasks.

Therefore, until the new testing systems are in place for a few years, with successful data collection, the school-wide standardized testing results will need to be viewed as benchmarks against which subsequent years' results can be compared. These benchmark data can be used to determine future trends, and as indicators of how students are performing with the new standards and curriculum. Examples of literacy data that can be examined for trends over time include:

- writing samples;
- individual reading assessments such as *Basic Reading Inventory* (Johns, 2016)
- measures of oral language proficiency (such as state language tests for English learners based on the WIDA Standards or other language development standards);
- percentage of students not reaching, reaching, and exceeding benchmarks, as measured by basal benchmark assessments; and
- vocabulary growth as measured by vocabulary assessments (see Johns, 2016, as an example).

For schools that are not using basal reading programs, including middle and high schools, indicators such as content area vocabulary assessments, Informal Reading Inventories, writing samples, foundational skills assessments, and teachers' anecdotal records can be used.

Identify Key Questions and Possible Problems Related to Students' Literacy Achievement

The question-asking process, during and after data analysis, is at the heart of the inquiry-based needs assessment process. Of course, many more questions may arise when you analyze your school and/or district literacy data, and any and all questions can be documented and discussed. From these important questions and the discussions concerning them, the school literacy team begins to identify and narrow the scope of the literacy problems students might be having. Most likely, instructional issues will begin to emerge from these discussions, and because the school's needs assessment process is multifaceted and substantive, the literacy team can turn to other data to look for instructional patterns that might be related to the students' literacy difficulties.

HOW DO WE ENGAGE TEACHERS IN IDENTIFYING CONDITIONS AND CONTEXTUAL FACTORS CONTRIBUTING TO PROBLEMS?

We now turn to the stakeholders who are collectively responsible for students' literacy development: their teachers; support personnel (such as reading specialists, literacy coaches, special education teachers); administrators; parents; and the students themselves.

Drafting a Needs Assessment Instrument for Teachers, Support Personnel, Administrators, and Parents

The purpose of this needs assessment is the same as that for the previous needs assessment of student achievement: to collaboratively identify existing problems through the examination of needs and strengths related to a particular topic or issue. However, instead of looking exclusively at student achievement data, the literacy team is now going to look at data provided by the school's other stakeholders. As the school's literacy instructional team begins determining what should be included in this needs assessment, the following questions should be considered:

1. Exactly which of the school's stakeholders will be asked to complete the literacy instructional needs assessment?
2. Who will create and distribute the needs assessments to the school's stakeholders?
3. Who will tally responses from teachers and support personnel? From administrators? From parents? From students (if appropriate and relevant)?
4. Who will summarize teachers' strengths and areas of concerns?
5. Who will report the needs assessment data, and with whom will it be shared?
6. What is the time frame for collecting the stakeholders' needs assessment data?
7. What is the time frame for analyzing, summarizing, and reporting the data?
8. Where and how will the data be stored?
9. How will the literacy team ensure that self-reported data will be collected anonymously?
10. How will the literacy team ensure confidentiality of all personal data?

Being able to answer the preceding organizational questions at the beginning of data collection can save frustration, time, and energy later on in the process. In a collaborative, inquiry-based endeavor, everyone is equitably involved and everyone knows the plan ahead of time, so the process can run smoothly.

Information that can be included in a school's needs assessment of stakeholders is found in Figure 3.5. These examples provide a comprehensive look at the knowledge, beliefs, attitudes, and feelings of multiple stakeholders in elementary and secondary schools related to the literacy development of students. Depending on the scope of your needs assessments, you may choose to include all, some, or a few of these tools in your survey of the school's literacy program.

Figure 3.5. Examples of Needs Assessment Indicators for Stakeholders

1. Professional demographics of teachers, administrators, and support personnel
   a. Years of employment as teacher, specialist, or administrator
   b. Degrees held; teaching and/or administrative credentials attained
   c. Special training or expertise in approaches, methods, or programs (e.g., Reading Recovery, ESL/ESOL, special education, literacy specialist, coaching experience, etc.)
   d. Languages spoken
   e. Other pertinent information
2. Demographics of parent representatives
   a. Occupation
   b. Previous participation in school activities and/or committees
   c. Number of children attending the school
   d. Special talents or skills that can contribute to establishing and meeting goals
3. Methods for obtaining data from stakeholders
   a. Written surveys (questions with rubric numbers to circle; multiple-choice answers; and/or open-ended responses)
   b. Satisfaction surveys (Likert scales*, such as Strongly Agree to Strongly Disagree)
   c. Interviews (obviously, these cannot be anonymous)

*Likert scale: A survey tool that asks the respondent to choose among several (usually 5) potential responses. It is considered a bipolar scale, because the response range is between two extremes (e.g., Strongly Agree and Strongly Disagree; Highly Likely and Highly Unlikely; Highly Evident and Not Evident).

Because schools have different cultures, contexts, and constituencies, it is impossible to provide you with one needs assessment instrument that will work for all of your stakeholders. However, in order to give you an idea of what a needs assessment might look like, we have included the teachers' needs assessment that was completed by each of the stakeholders at Blue Falls High School (see Figure 3.6, p. 56).

Analyzing Stakeholders' Needs Assessment Data

You will find that analyzing data from a Likert scale survey is easier than analyzing written comments and reflections. If you have a huge high school, you may wish to stick to surveys with Likert scales and simply determine percentages of responses along the scale. If you're in a smaller school, we encourage you to include some short-answer questions in the survey simply to be able to "hear" a respondent's voice through his or her writing. There's little to no nuance in Likert scale responses, and when respondents fill them out they can do so quickly and, sometimes, with little or no thought. Therefore, if possible, take the extra time to include a few short-answer questions so you'll have more substantive data to analyze.

As with the students' needs assessment data, look for trends in the adult data. If a large number of respondents are providing the same or similar answers (maybe the identical response or one-point difference on the Likert scale), then you might have a trend, especially if you have crafted several questions or statements that might yield the same or nearly the same response. For example, read each of these findings from the BFHS needs assessment data:

- 73% of the teachers and 80% of the literacy coaches reported that there are sufficient copies of short expository texts to use for teaching students how to do close readings.
- 62% of the teachers reported that they lacked confidence about teaching and providing practice in close reading of complex texts.
- 35% of the teachers reported feeling confident about teaching the skills and strategies needed to read challenging textbook material.
- 57% of the teachers reported they would participate in professional learning that includes a focus on how to help their students more effectively read difficult texts.

Figure 3.6. Blue Falls High School Literacy Survey

To: BFHS teachers, instructional support staff, and parent representatives

From: Literacy Instructional Team

Re: Literacy Needs Assessment

As you know, we have been meeting over the past few weeks to determine how we can better meet the language and literacy needs of our students. In order to narrow the focus of our work, we ask that you complete (anonymously) this needs assessment. *Respond only to the statements that pertain to you.* Please be as honest as possible in your responses, and **drop completed surveys into the marked box in the staff room by NOVEMBER 12.** Thank you for your help!

I am a:	I have been an educator for:
____ Teacher	a. ___ 1–5 years
____ Instructional support staff	b. ___ 6–10 years
____ Administrator	c. ___ 11–15 years
____ Parent representative	d. ___ 16+ years

For the following statements, please indicate with a number (1–5) what best reflects your true feelings.

1 = Strongly Disagree; 2 = Disagree; 3 = Unsure/Unknown; 4 = Agree; 5 = Strongly Agree

Instructional Materials

____ Appropriate texts and supplementary materials are available for planning content lessons.

____ There is adequate technology support to meet teachers' and students' needs.

____ There are sufficient text materials to differentiate for the reading abilities of students.

____ I know where to access brief passages for teaching and providing practice in close readings (narrative and expository).

____ I know how to determine if a text is at the right reading level for general use by students.

____ I know what to do if a text seems too challenging for particular students.

____ I know what to do if a text seems too easy for particular students.

____ I know how to determine if a text is appropriate for close reading instruction and practice.

____ I have adequate access to literacy assessment instruments that I can use with students.

____ I believe that the literacy instructional materials in my child's classrooms are adequate and appropriate.

Figure 3.6. Blue Falls High School Literacy Survey (continued)

Literacy Instructional Practices

____ I feel confident in managing differentiated instruction to meet the literacy needs of students.

____ I'm able to informally assess students' literacy skills.

____ I know how to use students' literacy assessment information when planning lessons.

____ I know how to determine the academic language of my content area.

____ I know how to teach the academic language of my content area.

____ I have an adequate repertoire of instructional techniques for infusing literacy skills and strategies into lessons.

____ I feel confident in meeting the language and literacy needs of the English learners in my classroom.

____ I feel confident in meeting the language and literacy needs of students who struggle with reading.

____ I feel confident in teaching and providing practice with close readings of complex texts.

____ I feel confident in teaching students how to find supporting evidence in texts.

____ I feel confident in teaching students how to develop positions based on supporting evidence they find in texts.

____ I feel confident in teaching students how to engage in instructional conversations and discussions.

____ I feel confident in teaching students how to craft and support arguments in writing.

____ I understand what is required in the Common Core ELA Standards.

____ I feel confident in teaching to the Common Core ELA Standards.

____ I feel that I am adequately informed about the Common Core ELA Standards.

____ I feel that I am able to adequately interpret literacy assessment information that is provided about my child's strengths and needs.

____ I feel confident about the literacy instruction for my child.

____ I feel confident about my child's literacy development as related to the state Common Core ELA Standards.

Below, feel free to add comments or questions related to the language and literacy development of your students (and/or your children). Add additional paper, if needed.

- 72% of the parent representatives reported that there were adequate instructional materials for their children.
- 68% of the parent representatives reported they didn't feel confident that their children were prepared to meet the state ELA standards.

Do you see any trends emerging from these findings? Think for a moment about how you might state them. Might the trends be stated something like this?

> While the majority of BFHS teachers and literacy coaches acknowledge there are sufficient texts to use when teaching and providing practice with complex texts, the majority of teachers do not feel confident about teaching close reading skills and strategies. Further, the majority of teachers would welcome professional learning opportunities to feel better prepared to help their students read challenging texts.

It's important to note that trends are not conclusions, nor do they imply causality. They simply point out a tendency or inclination. The more data you have that lean toward a trend, the stronger the trend becomes. One way to make analysis of the data an easier prospect is to include several questions or statements in the needs assessment that address an issue that the team thinks may be problematic, based on their analysis of student data. For example, let's say that reading assessment data indicate that students in grade 5 are having difficulty with vocabulary found in complex texts. The team decides to include questions on the needs assessment in order to test their informal hypothesis that vocabulary instruction may have insufficient rigor to enable students to successfully read challenging texts. Questions such as the following might be included:

- What types of academic vocabulary are the most challenging for your students:
    1. content-related or subject-specific vocabulary;
    2. general academic or cross-curricular vocabulary;
    3. academic vocabulary that is multisyllabic;
    4. all of the above?
- What are some examples of academic vocabulary that your students find especially challenging?
- What type of instruction works best for teaching your students challenging academic vocabulary?

- What would help you more effectively teach challenging academic vocabulary?

In addition, including different variations of essentially the same question and then analyzing the responses to these questions provides a deeper check for the problem and a more refined picture of it. This can also reinforce an issue the team suspects may be a problem. If there are no clear indications from respondents' answers because they are spread across the Likert scale, then there probably is no apparent trend for that particular issue.

Identifying Questions and Problems Related to the School's Literacy Profile

Again, as with the student needs assessment data, during discussions of the needs assessment results, many questions will arise, and these should be recorded and discussed. From the questions, problems will emerge, and identifying them in writing is critical to the needs assessment process, because subsequently these will be the problems that will be addressed through professional learning activities (see Chapter 4).

Let's revisit the vignette to see the results of the Blue Falls High School literacy team's needs assessment and the questions and problems that emerged from the students' and stakeholders' response data.

Revisiting the Blue Falls High School Vignette

The needs assessment draft for the high school's stakeholders was reviewed and revised by the BFHS literacy team, with input from the district literacy instructional team, and the final needs assessment was written. It included:

- Survey statements for classroom teachers, support personnel (literacy specialists and coaches, special educator), administrators, and parents (see Figure 3.6);
- Forms and questions for teachers' self-reflection reports and logs;
- Small-group and individual interview questions for teachers and grade-level teams; literacy specialists; instructional leaders (such as grade-level coordinators and department chairs); parents; and representative students.

The BFHS team then divvied up the tasks, established a schedule and calendar for interviews and surveys, and began assessing the stakeholders' needs.

Following this work, the instructional leadership team met in subgroups to analyze the data and generate questions (see Figure 3.7). Two trends found in data analysis revealed the following problems for students:

1. While comprehension assessment data indicated satisfactory factual recall for most students, across the grades students had difficulty with inferencing, problem solving, and application of concepts to real-world problems;
2. Because of these shortcomings, students were probably not prepared to deal with the Common Core ELA Standards that require critical thinking, close reading, and using supportive evidence from the text.

Trends emerging from the analysis of the needs assessments from teachers indicated:

1. Difficulty with selecting texts and other instructional materials of different genres to enable cross-disciplinary instruction;
2. Difficulty with providing instruction at all levels that focuses on comprehension and critical thinking when reading complex texts; and
3. Difficulty with creating multiple forms of informal assessments that are time-efficient and useful for informing literacy instruction.

Of the three, teachers indicated that the second area, teaching with complex texts, was of the highest priority. This identified need corresponded to an analysis of student data that indicated students made few gains in reading when tested on complex texts, especially nonfiction texts specific to history, literature, and science.

In the following chapters, we describe how the Blue Falls district literacy team worked with the elementary and secondary school literacy teams to develop appropriate and effective professional learning activities for teachers, with the common goal of increasing students' comprehension skills and strategies aligned with the state ELA standards.

CONNECTIONS TO THE PRINCIPLES OF
EFFECTIVE PROFESSIONAL LEARNING

In this chapter we discussed a process of school-wide and, ultimately, district-wide assessment of both students' and teachers' strengths

Figure 3.7. BFHS Literacy Team Questions Derived During Data Analysis

1. Given that the grade 9 students, for the most part, have satisfactory literal comprehension, why are so many of them having problems with inferencing and critical reading?
2. Has this been a problem with these students over the years, or is this a new issue because of the increased complexity of texts students are being asked to read?
3. Could students' difficulty with inference and close reading in expository texts be due to insufficient academic language proficiency?
4. Could students' difficulty be due to insufficient knowledge of academic vocabulary?
5. Could students' difficulty be due to a lack of experience with informational and expository texts?
6. Could students' difficulty be due to inappropriate texts (such as too easy or too hard)?
7. Could students' difficulty be due to insufficient practice in reading challenging expository texts?
8. Could students' difficulty be due to how we're teaching students to read challenging texts?
9. Are these difficulties unique to the grade 9 students, or do they exist across the high school?

and problems as related to a particular curricular issue—in this case, comprehension and critical reading. The assessment process is *situated* in a district's classrooms at the elementary, middle, and high school levels, and varied stakeholders are involved in this *collaborative* process. Because it involves analyzing data from varied sources of information in order to have multiple indicators of a particular problem, the questions that emerge during the process are *substantive* in nature.

CONNECTIONS TO THE COMMON CORE STATE STANDARDS AND OTHER STANDARDS-BASED POLICIES

If you are working in a state that has not adopted the Common Core ELA Standards or your state has adapted them according to somewhat different literacy guidelines, the information in this chapter can easily be modified for your particular standards. All states have adopted rigorous literacy standards within the last few years, and what is common among them is increased rigor and a focus on critical, close reading and robust vocabulary development. Regardless of how standards may evolve over the next decade, effective professional learning for teachers, aligned with the standards, is here to stay.

Questions for Reflection

1. Why should a variety of stakeholders (teachers and support personnel, administrators, parents) be involved in the needs assessment process? What are some advantages and disadvantages of surveying a sample of educators and parents, rather than collecting data from all involved?

2. While we didn't include students in the needs assessment survey process, we did suggest that they could be involved in interviews. Older students in high school certainly have legitimate feelings about their education, and should be consulted about how and what they're taught. If you were to design interview questions for the students in your school, what would you like to ask? How do you think the students might respond?

3. Multiple assessment tools are needed to identify needs and strengths of both students and teachers, with the purpose of setting direction for subsequent professional learning. What kind of information do you think would be helpful to you and your colleagues for determining student and teacher strengths and needs related to literacy instruction in your own school? How do you think your current administrators would feel about administering a needs assessment to your school's stakeholders? If they're reluctant, how might you involve them in the design of the needs assessment instrument?

CHAPTER 4

Creating the Professional Learning Plan and Putting It into Action

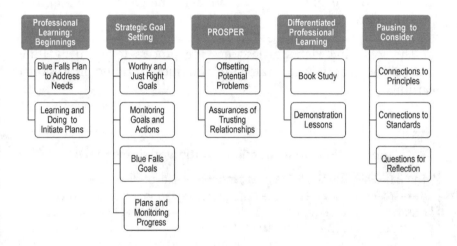

GETTING STARTED WITH PROFESSIONAL LEARNING

As we demonstrated in Chapter 3, there is much to be learned from a needs assessment that will shape the goals and professional learning activity. We approach professional learning as a process that invites educators (both administrators and classroom teachers), parents, and other stakeholders to generate questions and purpose for learning, and we expect that learning will occur in different ways and over time. It must be sustained to be meaningful and impactful. The process begins with goal setting and the development of a thoughtful plan, a plan that involves choice for teachers and opportunities for understanding the concerns and needs of every teacher, especially those teachers who may not be as forthcoming in expressing what worries them the most.

In this chapter and the one that follows, we provide examples of how educators use needs assessment data to make decisions about professional learning activities. Needs assessments lead to differentiated professional learning opportunities, as educators pursue those activities that are best suited to their questions and their needs. We also make connections in general to the actions of the Blue Falls K–12 educators. In this chapter, we focus more specifically on the middle school team, grades 5, 6, and 7.

We address two questions that the Blue Falls educators are asking:

- How can we be strategic when setting goals?
- How do we engage in professional learning within an inquiry framework?

The following vignette describes the process followed by Blue Falls educators as they generated their questions for their professional learning.

Connections to Instruction: Continuing the Vignette

The Blue Falls educators are analyzing the results of their needs assessment as they design their professional learning activities. These results were shared and discussed at a district-wide meeting and several meetings held at the school level.

Starting with the positive: Educators in this district, recently and before this new initiative to address the Common Core State Standards, made substantial progress learning about and teaching the STEM subjects and making connections across science, technology, engineering, and mathematics with a greater emphasis on the STEM subjects in the upper grades (grades 4 through 12). An examination of students' performance in the upper grades revealed steady progress in students' acquisition of academic vocabulary and concepts in the STEM subjects.

Needs assessment: Several needs related to text comprehension and deeper learning were revealed. The Blue Falls educators identified a need to strengthen students' text comprehension across the grades. A majority of students had basic understandings but were not fluent with the academic concepts taught in the STEM courses or had difficulty applying this information to real-world problems. Students across the grades had below-average performance on measures of inference, problem solving, and application.

Also, teachers reported dissatisfaction with the curriculum; it did not make explicit connections across the academic areas and the English language arts. They were interested in learning how to teach with more of an interdisciplinary focus and the use of added resources (e.g., informational texts and media).

One motivator for many Blue Falls educators, on their first viewing of the CCSS and before their needs assessments, was the belief that the CCSS adopted by the state represent substantive direction for improving curriculum and instruction while providing access to academic learning for all students. That direction coincides with their former work with STEM, where there was an emphasis on science, technology, engineering, and mathematics with the added benefit of integrating the English Language Arts.

Consider how you could use the needs assessment data to guide goals for professional learning, and consider the questions that the Blue Falls teachers were generating:

1. How will we set goals?
2. What process will facilitate achieving those goals?
3. What methods might advance our learning and thinking about teaching?

With the purpose of the chapter established, let's get started with the process of problem solving to set goals. From there, we discuss two professional learning activities and their connections to professional learning principles and state standards. We conclude this chapter with reflection questions.

HOW CAN WE BE STRATEGIC WHEN SETTING GOALS?

Problems and Needs Are Identified—Now What?

Moving from a needs assessment to goals and actions is the most exciting aspect of professional learning, or at least that is what *we* think of the steps of initiating and following a professional learning plan.

As educators, we create the plan. We are at the center of generating what we need to accomplish and how we want to proceed. This is not your mother's form of professional development, where top-down decisions or state-level mandates direct actions. Instead, inquiry-centered professional learning activity "favors ownership over compliance, conversation over transmission, deep understandings over enacting rules and routines, and goal directed activity over content coverage" (Raphael, Vasquez, Fortune, Gavelek, & Au, 2014, p. 147).

Returning to the Problem Solving as an Inquiry Process concept (Figure 1.4) introduced in Chapter 1, we are now focusing on the Learning and Doing strategies, as we will in Chapter 5 as well.

As we illustrate in Figure 4.1, there are questions that relate to maximizing educators' involvement in goal setting, plans for learning, and applications of new ideas to teaching.

Setting Worthwhile Goals

Specific features of goal setting that "matter the most" for influencing the learning and practices of teachers and students (Desimone, 2011; Steeg & Lambson, 2015; Garet et al., 2001) are displayed in Figure 4.2.

These features situate professional learning in solving authentic problems with a focus on knowledge development. They involve educators at all levels (i.e., administrators and classroom teachers, specialists and curriculum leaders) taking an active role in learning opportunities by meeting regularly and over time to build shared assumptions and expectations, and goals are explicit and monitored for progress. This process attends to three of our principles for professional learning—it is *intense, situated,* and *collaborative.*

Just Right Goals—Not Too Many, Not Too Few

Identifying the most appropriate goals begins the process for developing a professional learning plan that has universal support—educators can embrace it because it "feels" right. As we illustrate in Figure 4.3, the *just right* feeling comes from very deliberate decision-making.

We identify six decisions that move the process through goal setting, implementing the professional development plan, and monitoring learning and goal attainment. The first three decision points move the process from needs identification to goal setting. First, there are the decisions that represent the outcomes of the needs assessment,

Figure 4.1. Professional Learning as an Inquiry Process

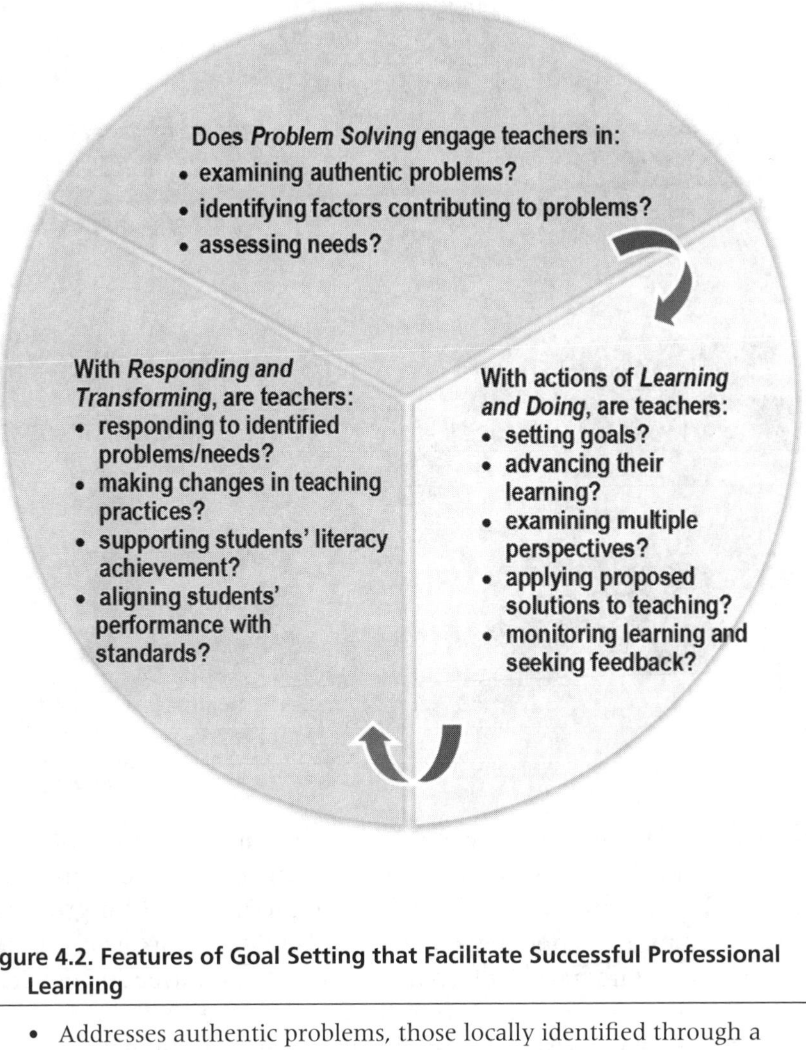

Does *Problem Solving* engage teachers in:
- examining authentic problems?
- identifying factors contributing to problems?
- assessing needs?

With *Responding and Transforming*, are teachers:
- responding to identified problems/needs?
- making changes in teaching practices?
- supporting students' literacy achievement?
- aligning students' performance with standards?

With actions of *Learning and Doing*, are teachers:
- setting goals?
- advancing their learning?
- examining multiple perspectives?
- applying proposed solutions to teaching?
- monitoring learning and seeking feedback?

Figure 4.2. Features of Goal Setting that Facilitate Successful Professional Learning

- Addresses authentic problems, those locally identified through a needs assessment and not mandated by external sources
- Assures coherence with the vision of the school and community network
- Focuses on knowledge development of students and teachers
- Invites active and collective teacher participation and learning
- Builds and advances shared assumptions
- Provides sustained engagement over time
- Shows progress in explicit and measurable ways

Figure 4.3. Deliberate Decision-Making for Goal Setting and Monitoring

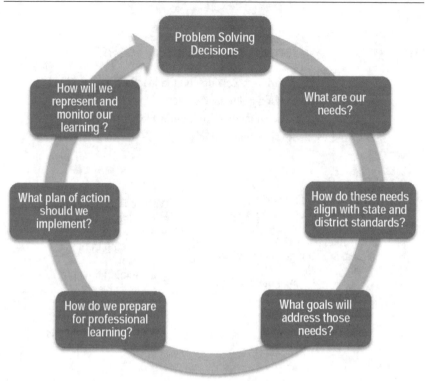

as described in Chapter 3, when analyzing multiple sources of information (student, instructional, and curricular strengths and problems and conditions contributing to each). We find it helpful for groups at the district and/or school level to chart this information, as illustrated in Figure 4.4, with a partially completed chart of information generated by the educators in one Blue Falls school.

The next two decisions focus on alignment with standards prior to setting goals. The goals, then, correspond directly to the needs information and standards-setting expectations for students' performance in the English language arts and the disciplines. Goal setting, decision three, acts as the "ignition" for the professional development pathway. Goals are well-defined, manageable, and measurable.

Typically, getting to the *just-right* goals for each year of the professional learning activity starts with a statement of a long-term goal. More than one long-term goal can be generated, but one goal, stated

Figure 4.4. Charting Strengths, Problems, Conditions, and Needs (Blue Falls Example)

Strengths	Problems	Conditions	Needs	Standard	Timeline for Instruction
Student learning – strong factual recall	Student Learning – limited attention to higher levels of comprehension, academic learning	Time blocks for extended student engagement	Develop higher levels of comprehension, access to academic content, engagement with academic texts		
Instructional – emphasis on text recall	Instructional – guided text readings inadequate – limited conceptual connections across ELA and disciplines	Limited strategies for integrating curriculum	Learn instructional strategies to meet needs of students; making connections across disciplines, close reading, higher levels of comprehension. Time for teams to plan for changes in instruction.		
Curricular – wide literary reading choices	Curricular – academic textbooks not accessible (lacking engaging content)	Limited access to text sets, text/content connections.	Identify and secure resources to support cross-curricular teaching		

broadly, typically provides a kick-start for setting more specific goals and corresponding time periods for completing each.

Methods for Goal Setting

We describe three methods that can be implemented to initiate the goal setting.

Backward mapping. One place to begin the process of goal setting is to start by engaging the school community (educators in the school district, students, and parents/community members) in generating a common vision of student learning outcomes or content learning or academic discipline goals. This backward-mapping process begins generally and addresses questions such as *what do we want our students to know and do as literate learners, as writers, as scientists, as historians?* This approach begins at a place where educators use their knowledge and expertise to generate ideas that are in their own words and work backward to establish goals and methods that will support the expected outcomes. This action is seen as particularly important for establishing dialogue and widespread participation in the process (Raphael et al., 2014).

Analyzing student data. As described in Chapter 3, another method for goal setting is to start with student data, typically data that are identified at the school or district level. *What are the areas where students across the grades are performing as expected, vs. areas that remain flat from year to year or are identified as weak?* Rather than backward mapping from a vision of what students should be able to do as graduates (or at designated levels in their education) and then aligning this vision with specific student data, educators start with the student data to provide information for identifying learning objectives (Firestone & Mangin, 2014) that are also aligned with adopted standards. With the analysis of student data, educators organize their professional learning around specific learning objectives they have for their students.

Generating visions of instruction. This method focuses on establishing a shared vision of instruction. For example, the Hermosa Elementary School (Steeg & Lambson, 2015) generated a shared vision of balanced literacy instruction and mentored new teachers by sharing their history of success and jointly refining how to teach within this vision. Educators may initiate the visioning process by describing instruction during which they felt most successful in engaging students in their learning, forms of instruction that supported students who had difficulties, or methods that address simultaneously all areas of the English language arts. Through this activity, educators learn whether or not they share a common vision, and if not, come together to construct a shared vision that represents the different views.

Educators can choose more than one of the above methods, as our Blue Falls example that follows illustrates. What is central to each, though, is the engagement of educators who are planning their future in professional learning. There are at least two outcomes of the goal setting process: Goals became more refined and precise through teamwork and collaboration, and shared learning among educators and the community develops common language and understandings about instructional methods and student learning goals.

**Connections to Goal Setting:
Continuing the Vignette**

Blue Falls' Process for Goal Setting—An Example

The Blue Falls educators used both student data and backward-mapping methods to generate their goals, starting with a broad goal statement and moving to more specific goals that were assigned to subsequent years within a three-year period.

As we reported in the vignette at the beginning of this chapter, the Blue Falls needs assessment revealed that higher levels of comprehension, including the skills of providing evidence to support interpretations and conclusions, and comprehending complex concepts often embedded in informational texts, were a challenge for students across the grades. And as we learned in Chapter 3, the majority of high school teachers, in particular, identified this problem in their needs assessments. These areas aligned with state and district standards emphasizing the development of student ability to draw conclusions, form argumentation with supporting evidence, and comprehend complex concepts across disciplines. The process, as demonstrated by the Blue Falls educators, begins with student needs and then is broadened to identify alignment between standards and student needs for long-term objectives.

At school-wide and district-wide meetings, educators generated their hopes for their students' learning, and this led to a statement of a general goal—*students will be able to read and comprehend (using recall, inferences, interpretations, and critical thinking) complex literary and informational-disciplinary texts*.

This conclusion led them to the backward-mapping process. First they did their homework by reading the work of Raphael et al. (2014) as an illustration of how a network of middle school and high school teachers, the Project READi Teacher Network in the Chicago schools, supported by a research project (Goldman et al., 2009), used backward mapping to develop their vision of cross-disciplinary teaching. Within that vision these educators generated outcomes they expected for high school graduates.

Next, the Blue Falls K–12 teachers initiated their own backward-mapping process. They met at the school level for three hours on Friday afternoons for three weeks at the beginning of the school year. They met in grade-level teams one week, disciplinary teams the second week, and then in a school-wide meeting the third week. At the first meeting, the teams generated their visions for what they wanted their students to learn in the English language arts and the academic disciplines. Then each disciplinary team generated its vision and a set of standards corresponding to what each student should learn at every grade level to meet those expectations.

At the third meeting, educators at each school came together and reflected on the listing of expectations for grade levels, for disciplines, and for the standards—presented in three columns on several charts, by grade level. From this listing, the general goal, and grade-level goals that were more specific, were aligned with standards per grade level.

Moving into grade-level teams, they assigned tasks for a 3-year period, for example, for the middle school level:

- In the first year, focus on goals for building comprehension at the various levels with text sets that make connections across literary texts and social studies texts. (Writing for argumentation and refutation was established as a first-year goal with connections to science.)
- In the second year, make connections for science and literary content.
- In the third year, use math concepts and other disciplinary concepts for solving real-world problems related to economics, conservation and ecology, and social studies.

HOW DO WE PREPARE FOR PROFESSIONAL LEARNING?

We want educators and their students to PROSPER with inquiry-based professional learning. Once initial goals are identified, it is important to offset potential problems while putting a plan into action, addressing question 4 of the decision-making process (as shown in Figure 4.3 [p. 68]). Our use of PROSPER as an acronym helped us to organize all the parts that go into preparing and sustaining learning. These elements represent the infrastructure and the foundation for professional learning efforts:

Purpose is established
Responsibilities are assigned
Organization of space and time is set
Safety nets are generated
Problems are identified
Examples are identified
Repetition through iterative cycles advances progress

The ***Purpose*** for each small- or large-group activity is identified explicitly at the beginning of each meeting and reviewed at the end of the session; this is a cyclical process, with the purpose set for subsequent meetings. For example, a team in a book study may set the purpose for generating three takeaway teaching implications from the book's first chapter. Purpose setting keeps the meeting on track, and is applied routinely for both formal and informal meetings (e.g., meeting at a local coffee shop after school).

Responsibilities are assigned to all team members. For some educators, being responsible for generating questions and guiding one's own learning is very different from years of passive involvement in professional development work. It is important for administrators and instructional leaders to provide multiple examples of the characteristics of inquiry-based professional learning (where educators are responsible for directing their learning) and to lead by example as they participate in district, school, or team meetings. Puzio, Newcomer, and Goff (2015), for example, describe principals as agents of change when they take an active role in networking teachers strategically. Classroom teachers and instructional leaders, often working jointly, may take on the role of discussion leader or note-taker. See Figure 4.5 (p. 74) for examples of responsibilities and roles assumed by team members.

Figure 4.5. Roles and Responsibilities

Tasks	School District Admin.	School Admin.	Curriculum/ Instructional Leaders	Literacy Coach	Classroom Teachers	Outside Consult/ University
Allocate space/time						
Make student data available						
Provide resources for data collection						
Establish networks						
Provide lesson demonstrations						
Create resource library						
Take notes						
Summarize						
Conduct peer observations						

Organization of space and time and using time well. Teachers
need assurances that there will be space reserved for their meetings,
time to concentrate on professional learning, and that the space and
time will be protected. Administrators at the district and school level
need to consult with teachers when organizing for meetings. There
may be a small number of district-wide meetings, with more frequent
meetings for educators at the school level. For example, at the district level, four Wednesdays spaced across the school year could be
established on the yearlong calendar for district-wide meetings. At the
school level, every third Wednesday afternoon is set aside for professional learning. Comfortable and flexible use of space is also important
to support various activities (e.g., lesson demonstrations, small-group
discussions) with access to whiteboards, computers, and other forms
of media to display work, access online materials, and keep records.

Creating ***Safety Nets*** to develop a culture of collegiality and respect
for different experiences and viewpoints is vital. These safety nets may
be the most important characteristic of PROSPER, for they signal to
teachers that they will be learning in a safe and supportive environ-
ment. They are explicit and typically are put in place by district- and
school-level administrators to:

- ***Assure teachers that they will be supported as they implement
  new practices.*** Teachers need to be assured that resources
  required for changes are available and that administrators will
  support new practices that are in development. Administrators
  who join in discussions of new directions are more likely to
  understand that learning new practices takes time, and that
  small steps forward can lead to longer-lasting changes.
- ***Respect anxiety about change.*** Teachers engaged in learning
  new instructional strategies may have difficulty applying
  what they have learned to their own classrooms. Teachers
  need to know they can request mentoring as they implement
  and evaluate new strategies. From the onset, administrators,
  especially principals and instructional leaders such as literacy
  coaches, should establish networks of mentors, including peer
  coaches (Puzio, Newcomer, & Goff, 2015).

Focus on Problems rather than on (judging) teachers. Within an
inquiry approach, building trust is essential and strategies for conflict
resolution and reaching consensus must be in place. Teachers need

to feel comfortable asking questions, explaining problems they see in their student data, and hypothesizing about possible changes and instructional moves. In some districts, teachers have data meetings throughout the year where all teachers and instructional leaders take turns sharing at least one challenge relevant to student data and requesting feedback and suggestions. A few teachers have told us that their anxiety about sharing their students' performance data quickly diminished once they felt the respect and support of their colleagues.

Examples in the form of written accounts, demonstrations, YouTube and other online videos, and visits to classrooms provide explicit applications of how new forms of instruction are implemented within authentic settings. There is much to notice in examples, and discussion of these provides opportunities for educators to identify specific details and generate possible connections and applications.

Repetition that involves multiple iterative cycles of reading professional resources and/or implementing, evaluating, and refining instruction deepens knowledge, and when knowledge increases, educators become more confident in their efforts to make changes that are useful for them and their students. Iterative cycles often provide contrast sets or alternate ways of proceeding, a powerful learning experience that contributes to flexible use of knowledge and abilities to adjust when instruction or student learning may not develop as planned. These cycles represent a sequence of inquiries, with the result of each informing the next (Bryk, Gomez, Grunow, & LeMahieu, 2015)

WHAT ARE PLANS FOR PROFESSIONAL LEARNING AND MONITORING PROGRESS?

Two additional questions guide the initial planning for professional learning: What plan of action should we implement, and how will we monitor our learning (questions 5 and 6 in Figure 4.3)? In the remainder of this chapter and in Chapter 5, we describe multiple ways in which educators participate in differentiated forms of professional learning. We provide examples of how these activities lead to actions that enhance learning and teaching, and more specifically we describe the actions that Blue Falls teachers enact to meet their goals. Through the process of engaging in professional learning, educators begin to lay out their theories of change—how they can apply what they are learning to their teaching—and specific procedures for those applications. To monitor their learning and progress toward meeting their goals, multiple forms of data are collected. For example, teachers may keep reflection journals, where they analyze what they are learning and their classroom applications. Additionally, peer observations, analyzing notes taken during data-sharing meetings, reviewing methods for refining instruction, and interviewing students provide data that are useful for monitoring progress and/or a need for revising actions.

WHAT ARE MULTIPLE PATHWAYS
FOR ENGAGING LEARNING AND DOING?

Once goals and a plan are developed, we enact PROSPER, with safety nets in place so that educators can move forward to participate in professional learning activities. These activities are differentiated to address needs and goals, and can include book study and lesson demonstrations (addressed in this chapter) and teacher research, family study groups, lesson study, and mentoring arrangements, including mentoring relationships with critical friends and literacy coaches (discussed in Chapter 5).

We begin our discussion by describing the book-study activity, one form of a collaborative teacher study group that is organized to deepen knowledge and encourage applications in practice. Often it is the first step in moving into other forms of professional learning, for, if done well, the book-study activity helps educators view instruction and understand students in new ways, examine their own instruction, and make changes in practices.

For each professional learning activity, we address these questions: What is it? Why would we use it? What steps should we follow to implement it? What is an example of the activity? What can we learn from the example? What are the challenges and implications?

BOOK STUDY

What is it? Book study brings educators together to choose and read professional texts—a single text, a series of texts, an article, or a series of articles. Texts are chosen based on educators' questions and specific problems; thus, these groups are often referred to as teacher or educator study groups.

Why would we use it? Book studies are particularly useful for building new and shared knowledge that is often required for meeting new goals and redesigning instruction and curriculum. Particularly effective are school-wide book-study groups that have small-group arrangements, with everyone in the school a member of a group. These groups may form as grade-level or cross-grade-level teams. Sharing across groups at regular intervals with particular attention to how content is tested in classrooms and discussing how educators in the group might apply ideas to their own practices are particularly important for deepening knowledge (Lick & Murphy, 2007).

What steps should we follow to implement it? Several procedures are required.

- *Forming groups.* Groups can be formed at different levels (e.g., whole school, small groups within school, grade-level groups across schools) and represent different areas (e.g., both classroom teachers and administrators within the same group or forming different groups). Each has advantages, but there are two caveats: Large groups limit participation, and less engagement may result in limited applications.
- *Clarifying expectations.* Establishing expected outcomes should lead to specific activities. For example, knowledge building and taking ideas to practice may require coupling book study with lesson demonstrations or other forms of professional learning that emphasize applications.
- *Choosing the text(s) to be read.* Literacy coaches, instructional leaders, peers, consultants, and/or university colleagues may recommend possible texts. Often more than one book is under consideration; book talks can be held to facilitate choices.
- *Reading the text(s).* Each group should decide how the book will be read (e.g., in small chunks) and the timeline for reading and preparing for group discussions.
- *Preparing for group discussion.* This typically involves note-taking and coding ideas from the readings. For example, Elish-Piper and L'Allier (2014) recommend that teachers prepare notes that include main ideas, questions about the readings, and ideas for applications. They describe methods for coding segments of texts, such as signaling important or confusing ideas, and for keeping journals, such as a double-entry journal with interpretations given for selected text ideas.

- *Structuring the discussions.* This involves a designated discussion leader for each session who not only moves the conversation along and keeps the focus on text content, but also plans for the session with a few opening questions and concludes the discussion with a brief summary and a suggested direction for subsequent discussion (Elish-Piper & L'Allier, 2014). One method of structuring book talks is to focus on applications for instruction with specific guiding questions, as shown in Figure 4.6.
- *Staying focused.* Structured book talks can be useful for keeping a focus on the specific issues under study, so that conversations don't run adrift with too much emphasis on problems without solutions (Birchak et al., 1998).
- *Distributing knowledge.* Organize a school- or district-wide method for sharing what is learned from the readings and applications. Group members may report on their work to other groups, sharing summaries of discussions and action steps. Such sharing is important for distributing knowledge across groups and building expertise.
- *Reflecting on learning at the end of each session.* Ask "What did I learn?" "How will I use this information?" "What do I expect the outcomes of my applications to be?"

Figure 4.6. Book Study Discussion Topics with a Focus on Instruction

Come to the discussion group, after reading a designated text piece, prepared for the following discussions. Perhaps you will choose a subset of these discussion points.

- Familiar. Choose and share one instructional strategy that is similar to strategies you use when teaching. Explain your procedures and their impact on students.
- Unfamiliar. Choose and share one instructional strategy that is new to you and discuss how you might implement it in your classroom. What do you expect to be the outcome?
- Identify questions you have about the reading, including possible confusions.
- Address a particular need. Identify one specific learning objective for your student(s). Then choose one strategy (familiar or unfamiliar) and explain how you will implement it and what its purpose is, identifying expected outcomes. Be prepared to invite questions and advice from team members.
- Reporting. Explain the forms of data (e.g., student data, peer observational data) you will collect and report on at a subsequent meeting.

What is an example of this activity? The Hermosa Elementary School provides one example of how book-study groups can be implemented.

Example. The Hermosa schools, introduced earlier in this chapter, decided to combine book study with lesson demonstrations. Before the groups began meeting, however, classroom teachers took the first months of the school year to focus on a close study of readers in their classrooms, developing case studies. Each teacher selected a student and collected formative data during conferences (e.g., recording oral reading miscue data, preferences and interests, comprehension of texts), developing a case study to take to small groups, reporting on observations and interpretations, seeking guidance from colleagues, and applying suggestions in the classroom. Topics of common interest (e.g., how to conference with readers, how to lead inquiry-based lessons, how to make connections between science and literature) were generated and matched to recommended professional readings.

Deliberate and specific procedures, as described above, were followed. A facilitator and timekeeper were chosen to monitor each discussion, keeping groups on topic and recording notes that were written afterward in brief summaries and shared with the team members. At the end of each book study session, the teachers wrote quick writes reflecting on the content and possible applications. The facilitators used the summaries and quick writes to facilitate the planning for the next meeting. Teachers took turns as facilitators.

What can we learn from the example? Engaging in a book study for professional learning is not a casual process. It should be purposeful and deliberate, and responsive to the inquiry in process. To influence teacher learning and content applications, discussions are intense; additional readings may be introduced to examine alternative perspectives, and members are held responsible for their contributions and their takeaways.

As illustrated with Hermosa, note-taking and follow-up questions facilitate future discussions. Applications and sharing of insights provide a careful study of the content. This intentional work engages community building for professional learning and clearly moves away from top-down leadership and mandates to group knowledge building and decision-making. Activities such as coding texts and discussing these codes, or selecting text chunks to be discussed, deepen knowledge and empower teachers to choose what is most relevant and helpful for their teaching.

What are the challenges and implications? The role of the discussion leader is extremely important for keeping group discussions on topic, engaging everyone in the discussion, and providing coherence within each meeting and when planning for the next session. Sharing leadership by turn-taking is one way to engage everyone's participation and ownership of the professional learning events. Protocols with questions such as "What am I learning?" and "How can I use this information in my teaching?" are useful for guiding discussions and applications.

Typically, several professional texts are read in concert with one another, and often these readings provide different perspectives or pathways for applying research and practical ideas. As we noted earlier, iterative cycles that engage teachers in the study of different viewpoints are particularly useful for deepening knowledge and building expectations for flexible use of information that is needed for solving problems.

LESSON DEMONSTRATIONS

What is it? A lesson demonstration, as the name implies, provides a live example of an instructional event, with an opportunity to question and analyze what is modeled. Demonstrations are used to revisit and refine current practices or to illustrate new forms of instruction. These may enact a complete lesson or components of a lesson. Demonstrations, typically occurring within a real classroom setting, provide an up-close view of teaching and student learning as they occur. Demonstrations are rich with information and opportunities, providing multiple layers of activity simultaneously (e.g., class organization, texts in use, teacher and student talk, and so on) that can be analyzed from different perspectives (e.g., appropriateness of text or assignment, impact of teacher talk, nature of student talk, and so on).

Why would we use it? Demonstrations are chosen for multiple reasons. First, educators have an opportunity to observe how the ideas work in their real world of teaching. And as they view teaching in action, they can see explicit instructional actions. Second, as educators observe student engagement and learning, they come to understand the impact of the instruction on students. Firestone and Mangin (2014) refer to demonstrations as *existence proofs* when these demonstrations include authentic examples or "proofs" of how children are learning within the targeted instruction. Observing a positive impact on student engagement and learning can be a powerful motivator for educators, and after viewing effective demonstrations, it is more likely that teachers will apply these ideas to their own practice (Firestone & Mangin, 2014).

Third, as Joyce and Calhoun (2014) noted, demonstrations are particularly powerful for building teacher knowledge (i.e., of the rationale, how goals are met, and procedures for engaging both teachers and students in dynamic learning experiences). Such engagement can have a dramatic effect on the likelihood of implementation that is sustained. Joyce and Calhoun reported that up to 90% of their teachers implemented targeted instruction when those conditions were met, as compared to about a 10–15 % rate of implementation when only one of those elements was present.

What steps should we follow? Typically, these procedures are implemented.

- *Setting goals.* Goals for content learning and instruction are matched to the question "What do we need to know and do to meet our instructional goals?"
- *Building knowledge.* There is usually some professional reading on the topic and a conclusion by team members to observe an explicit demonstration of the intended instruction.
- *Identifying the demonstration teacher.* The team, perhaps guided by the school's literacy coach, will identify who might provide the demonstration. Literacy coaches, teacher leaders or teachers within the district, invited consultants (e.g., a teacher from another school district brought in as a consultant), and/ or university faculty who are collaborating with the school district may provide the lesson demonstrations; or these can be provided by web-supported access to videos of instruction.
- *Conducting pre- and post-demonstration discussions.* Prior to teaching, goals and procedures are shared; these are reviewed and analyzed in the discussion that follows.

- *Including iterative cycles,* if needed. Iterative cycles may be needed for refinement and adaptations.
- *Reflecting on learning at the end of each session.* Ask "What did I learn?" "How will I use this information?" "What do I expect the outcomes of my applications to be?"

What is an example of this activity? Our example comes from a lesson demonstration described by Priscilla Griffith and her colleagues.

Example. Educators in an Oklahoma school invited a teacher from another district who was known for successfully integrating reading and writing in her 5th-grade classroom when teaching with informational texts (Griffith, Plummer, Connery, Conway, & Wade, 2014). Prior to conducting her lesson, the consultant studied the school's curriculum and the teachers' goals. As she began her lesson demonstration in a classroom, she shared a graphic organizer of her lesson components. After the lesson, she and the teachers constructed a chart addressing questions such as "What did I do and why?" "How did I do it?" and "What did it look like?" Together the educators and consultant deconstructed the lesson, drawing attention to its details. The consultant and the observers could have asked additional questions about teacher decision-making and adjustments made during the lesson based on student participation. Or they could have generated questions about teacher talk (e.g., How did the teacher set up the lesson? How did the teacher invite engagement and student talk?) or student talk (e.g., Did students generate their questions and interpretations, and have opportunities to share their thinking or writing?).

Student work was collected and analyzed during the post-demonstration discussion. A writing rubric of good writer traits was taught and applied to the writing samples. Six additional lessons were conducted across the year, with each lesson focusing on a different aspect of writing across literacy and social studies, and subsequent questions and goals generated by the teachers. At the conclusion of each lesson, educators were asked to name one idea they took away from the demonstration and how this idea might relate to their teaching goals.

What can we learn from the example? There is much to learn from this example. The lesson construction chart and the graphic organizer provided explicit information about the lesson components, and with the discussion around the lesson construction, educators constructed understandings of rationale, procedural information, and quality of teacher and student participation. At the teachers reflected on what they were learning, they generated connections between these lessons and their own teaching.

What are the challenges and implications? Lesson demonstrations are teacher-friendly, providing authentic events and opportunities to engage analysis and reflection before application. Yet they can have limited impact if they are provided only once and/or within one context (e.g., a writing lesson demonstrated within a 5th-grade language arts context may not apply easily to a 7th-grade social studies lesson). Thus, several iterations across the school year, demonstrated by educators with different areas of expertise and across several content and grade-level contexts, would heighten usability and knowledge building.

Demonstrations can serve as an anchor for further study, as they are rich with information for building shared knowledge relating to local goals and vision. This is especially useful for teachers who come to professional learning with diverse histories, knowledge, and expectations. And with iterations at different grade levels and in different content areas, educators can contrast potential implications for differentiating applications; thus the study of contrast sets is also important for deepening knowledge.

Demonstrations may be especially useful when combined with other forms of learning. For example, the Hermosa school system began each professional learning session with a mini lesson demonstration or a lecture (Steeg & Lambson, 2015), followed by large- and small-group discussions and reading of professional texts. They followed lesson demonstrations with applications that they called "Try IT," and informal reporting back to their groups.

CONNECTIONS TO THE PRINCIPLES
OF EFFECTIVE PROFESSIONAL LEARNING

As we come to this place in our chapter, you might be asking "What is new about these forms of professional learning?" Perhaps you have experienced these forms of professional learning in top-down and administrator-initiated approaches. Here is what's different: Educators at all levels initiate a specific activity, and it is *their* questions that are addressed in each. Each professional learning activity provides intense focus on question generation and problem solving—one principle of our professional learning paradigm. Second, each is situated within the purpose and intended outcomes identified by the educators at the school and/or district levels. And, in keeping with our third principle, each invites collaborative and supportive environments for learning.

As with the Hermosa School District decisions, these forms of professional learning activities can be coupled to deepen knowledge— going beyond printed explanations and descriptions to view the application. Planning for more than one iteration of either or both provides for sustained and intensive learning. And it reinforces the importance of learning different perspectives. Thus, readings on the same topic but written to represent different viewpoints, or lesson demonstrations that have the same goals and outcomes but different setups and development, are also important for building expertise (Sabers, Cushing, & Berliner, 1991). These contrasting sets help educators notice details and learn to interpret reasons for actions and the multidimensional layers of teaching and learning (Merriman, 2014).

Lesson demonstrations can also be coupled with visits to classrooms in or outside the district, or with online videos of similar demonstrations, each observation extending knowledge so that educators can examine how the instruction is applied at different grade levels, to meet different purposes or needs of students. For example, one group of Blue Falls middle school teachers requested two sets of lesson demonstrations—one set focused on strategies for integrating writing within social studies lessons and the second set on teaching writing for argumentation. The teams met weekly, first to discuss the demonstrations and to map out their own applications, and second to share their observations and recommendations for refining their instruction.

CONNECTIONS TO THE COMMON CORE STATE STANDARDS AND OTHER STANDARDS-BASED POLICIES

New knowledge is needed for moving in new directions. The knowledge development for addressing the Common Core State Standards (and similar standards adopted by states) requires specialized forms of knowing, on multiple levels. At the lowest level of engagement and learning, educators must examine current curricula and instruction, along with their relationship to new standards and expectations for what is required for teaching these new standards (e.g., perhaps close rereading is a new concept to the school district and will require attention in adjusting and implementing new forms of instruction). Note that the Blue Falls educators concluded early on that there was a lack of congruence between their curriculum and the adopted new standards, setting a need for working toward this alignment.

At a higher level is the knowledge required for implementing new practices, such as integrating the English Language Arts and academic content. Typically such integration requires much more than a simple tinkering with what is already in place. Integration may require extensive and prolonged study of the structure and conceptual elements of academic content, how students learn in these areas, and instructional methods that facilitate such learning (Merriman, 2014). The Blue Falls teachers began to engage in these deeper forms of learning with their book-study groups and lesson demonstrations. In particular, the middle school teachers focused their attention on how to implement writing instruction to engage students' close reading of social studies texts with activities such as noting critical incidents in history, how historians wrote about these incidents, and writing from a historian's perspective with the genre/structure of the discipline.

Questions for Reflection

1. Professional development leader and researcher F. M. Newman (1996) argued that five characteristics—developing shared values and norms, focusing on student learning, providing opportunities for reflection and dialogue among educators, collaborating as an expected activity, and teaching made public—must be present if we expect professional learning to occur. Examine each of these characteristics and determine whether this set is embedded in book study and lesson demonstrations. How so, and if not, what would need to occur to ensure optimal conditions?

2. Reread the PROSPER elements and think about what might have surprised you. Which ones are most relevant to your school and teaching situations? What, if anything, would you add?

3. Think about the pleasure-reading book clubs in which you have participated and how a group focusing on professional texts might differ from one reading favorite fictional/nonfictional texts. What strategies might carry over from your experiences as a book club member? What strategies might you adopt in a professional book-study group, and what would you expect from other group members?

CHAPTER 5

Sustaining the Professional Learning Plan

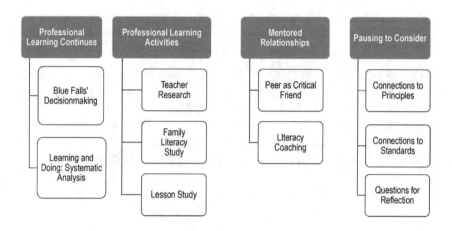

The Blue Falls Pre-K–4 educators, as described below, are tackling difficult issues as they learn about new standards for integrating the curriculum and focus on methods to address students who are experiencing literacy difficulties. These are challenges that each of us has faced as classroom teachers, reading specialists, and literacy coaches. And they are challenges for teachers at all levels in the Blue Falls District. We know there is no one right way to proceed, but we have learned that a systematic analysis of our teaching and our students' learning can make all the difference in our problem solving.

Connections to Instruction: Continuing the Vignette

The Blue Falls educators are engaged in differentiated professional learning activities. Guided by their peers, instructional leaders, and their own questions and concerns, educators (administrators, instructional leaders, literacy coaches and specialists, and classroom teachers) are choosing and joining groups to develop knowledge and direction for instruction that will meet their school-wide goals for the next 3 years (i.e., integrating reading and writing and social studies with complex texts, including developing writing for argumentation in year 1; integrating literacy and science instruction with complex texts in year 2; and applying academic concepts to solving real-world problems in year 3). An emphasis on critical thinking and deeper learning is embedded in their 3-year goals.

Early in the process, classroom teachers begin to generate specific questions that they have about their own teaching as they express concerns about applications of new teaching ideas and what impact these applications may have on their students' literacy and academic learning. The administrators, including team leaders and literacy coaches, at each school engaged in specific professional learning activities. At times they formed administrative groups, but often the literacy coaches joined teams mostly comprised of teachers.

The Pre-K–4th grade team of teachers were concerned about the students who continued to struggle with reading and writing across the early grades. They had attended a state literacy conference and heard a speaker who argued that school improvement plans were incomplete if they did not involve families in the process. And they examined the national policy Every Student Succeeds Act (2015), which draws specific attention to low-performing schools and students who are traditionally underserved.

As we reflect on the concerns of these teachers in the early grades, we identify questions that will be addressed in this chapter. These questions are central to professional learning, as they serve to deepen teachers' analytical problem solving and ability to make meaningful changes in instruction.

1. What professional learning activities are particularly useful in helping teachers examine students' learning and/or lesson components systematically?
2. How can teachers use professional learning activities to engage parents in meaningful conversations about literacy and learning in and out of school, and then apply what is learned to their teaching?
3. How can peers and literacy coaches support teachers in ways that address individual and personal concerns?

ADDITIONAL PATHWAYS
FOR ENGAGING LEARNING AND DOING

In this chapter we identify professional learning activities—teacher research groups, family literacy study groups, lesson study, and mentoring, as provided by peers and/or literacy coaches—that are particularly useful for inviting careful and analytical thinking about problems we face. They address the learning and doing questions represented in Figure 5.1, and in our concept of *Professional Learning as an Inquiry Process*. As with book study and lesson demonstrations, discussed in the previous chapter, each activity is designed to deepen professional knowledge and facilitate applications that are optimal for effective

Figure 5.1. Professional Learning as an Inquiry Process

Does *Problem Solving* engage teachers in:
- examining authentic problems?
- identifying factors contributing to problems?
- assessing needs?

With *Responding and Transforming*, are teachers:
- responding to identified problems/needs?
- making changes in teaching practices?
- supporting students' literacy achievement?
- aligning students' performance with standards?

With actions of *Learning and Doing*, are teachers:
- setting goals?
- advancing their learning?
- examining multiple perspectives?
- applying proposed solutions to teaching?
- monitoring learning and seeking feedback?

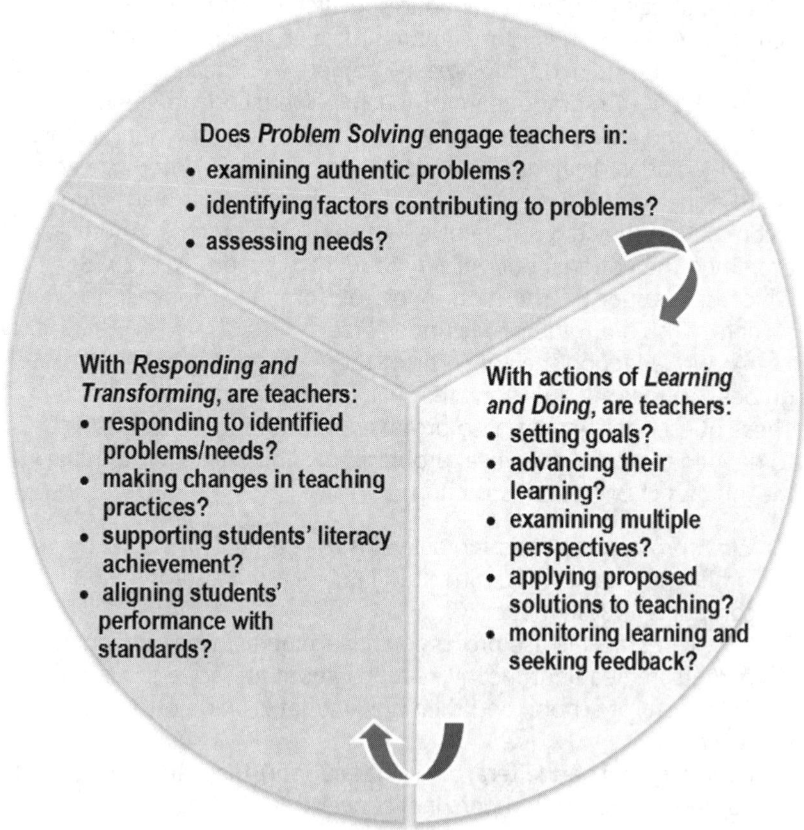

instruction and student engagement and learning. At the end of this chapter we discuss how sustaining a commitment to the activities is important for implementing changes that have the most impact on our teaching and our students' learning.

The methods described in this chapter require a systematic approach to our inquiry and problem solving. We provide examples that apply to all grade levels with a specific focus on Pre-K–4 grades. We continue to address the question "How do we engage professional learning within an inquiry framework?" with the added questions of "What methods invite parents into our learning process and what methods can address our individual needs?" Professional learning, as we demonstrate in this chapter, is *dynamic, intense, situated, substantive, collaborative,* and *personal.*

As we turn to a new set of professional learning activities, we remind ourselves that each will be optimal once we have assured ourselves that the PROSPER elements, including the safety nets, are in place. With PROSPER, we, as educators, can trust that the Purpose for our work is established, Responsibilities are assigned, Organization of space and time is set, Safety nets (of building trust and respect for anxiety) are generated, Examples are identified, and Repetition to advance progress is in the plan (see Chapter 4 for further discussion of these elements). And we can expect that our professional learning is developing within collegial and trusting relationships.

TEACHER RESEARCH

What is it? Teacher research engages all the processes of inquiry learning—identifying specific problems and questions, collecting and analyzing data, modifying conditions and practices, analyzing modifications, and refining instruction. One teacher may initiate a teacher research project by focusing on his/her own teaching questions and then collaborating with others during implementation, or it may be initiated and implemented school- or district-wide (Check & Shutt, 2012). Action research, a form of teacher research, has the added requirement of multiple inquiry cycles to refine the questions, data gathering and analysis process, and outcomes.

Why would we use it? A focused inquiry can deepen knowledge about conditions contributing to problems, such as problems students experience with reading comprehension, and identify how changes in instruction might impact learning in new ways (Check & Shutt, 2012). Over time and with continued practice, teachers become more analytical about their practices; teacher research is associated with professional growth and transformed instruction (Cochran-Smith & Lytle, 2001).

What steps should we follow? Teacher research involves the following procedures:

- *Building knowledge.* Two types of professional readings support knowledge development. One type focuses on research methods for posing explicit questions, collecting and analyzing data, and reporting findings; the second type focuses on content.
- *Generating specific questions.* Specific questions guide observations and data collection (e.g., "How will my close reading instruction support the learning of James, who has difficulty comprehending the social studies textbook?" Or "How can this instruction involve other students?") Questions may be modified when the data suggest a more specific direction.
- *Collecting data.* Some measures are student-based (e.g., comprehension measures, interviews with student), some instruction-based (e.g., recording teacher-student talk ratios), and some assist the teacher's analysis (e.g., protocols for note-taking, a teacher journal to report observations, audio- or videotaped lessons). A protocol for note-taking, for example, could have separate columns for observations, interpretations, and action steps.
- *Allocating time for research.* Estimate how many lessons may be needed to accomplish objectives.
- *Planning for observations and dialogue.* Invite peer observers and set up data-sharing meetings to interpret findings and plan instruction.
- *Addressing validity and ethical issues.* For validity, plan to collect several forms of data over time, cross-referencing data points to identify patterns and support interpretations. For ethical considerations, follow school procedures for assuring confidentiality of participants and seeking approval of participants.

- *Reporting of findings.* Sharing across groups distributes new knowledge to peers.
- *Reflecting on learning.* Ask "What did I learn?" "How will I use this information?" "What do I expect the outcomes of my applications to be?"

What is an example of this activity? One example is the project-based research activity implemented by Rye, Rummel, Forinash, Minor, and Scott (2015). They investigated the impact of garden-based learning on students' science and math learning at North Elementary School in Morgantown, WV. Students were engaged in a yearlong project in which they used math and science principles for designing gardens and crop plantings and recording yield and nature of products. Along the way they read numerous informational and procedural texts and novels about plant growth, integrating the English language arts into the instruction. The year began with an idea about the benefits of a garden project, offered by James Rye, a West Virginia University science professor who partnered with the school. Teachers began to talk about authentic ways for their students to apply what they were learning to gardening projects, and students generated questions when reading puzzling or incomplete information, such as how to produce and care for strawberries all year in a climate that can be harsh in the winter. Families were involved in the planting and data collection with at-home projects. Students wrote daily about their observations and included data to support their interpretations. Findings indicated that students were learning argumentation and how to use precise measurements to support their conclusions, and concepts were applied to the design and implementation of new projects.

What can we learn from the example? In this example, educators are not just solving problems, but posing questions to direct research on their own practices and student learning. This approach is consistent with a scientific method applied to teaching, in which teachers take responsibility for changing situations, not just interpreting them (Kemmis & McTaggart, 1988). Multiple forms of data collection and opportunities for peer feedback and dialogue can contribute to teachers' confidence in their decisions and help them take ownership of their professional learning (Youngs & Lane, 2014). As Rye and his colleagues demonstrate, project-based learning that invites cycles of investigative questions and allows redesigning of the project can be a robust form of instruction; it enhances teacher and student learning as well as family involvement.

What are the challenges and implications? Time may be needed at the startup for building knowledge, especially of research methods. Yet some teachers will have had this preparation from their teacher education or advanced certification programs. Teachers who have participated in the National Writing Project, for example, bring this knowledge with them to a teacher research project. They typically have a history of generating and reporting on research projects and receiving technical and methodology support at their national meetings (Check & Shutt, 2012).

Knowledgeable others (e.g., teachers from other school districts, instructional leaders for the district, university professors) who can support professional learning and the research process may be needed, especially in the initial stages. This involvement seems to be most helpful when these individuals join the teacher research team (e.g., James Rye, in the above example) to develop shared knowledge and expectations.

FAMILY LITERACY STUDY GROUP

What is it? This study group aligns with the practices of teacher research groups, but there is a specific emphasis on gaining knowledge about students' families and communities. Educators may want to know more about the literacy events students experience outside of school (Mui & Anderson, 2008), the languages used in the homes of multilingual families, or parents' expectations for their students' literacy achievement. In turn, parents often want to know about the school's goals for their children. A representative group of parents may be part of the planning team.

Why would we use it? We believe that goals for professional learning and improving instruction cannot succeed without parent involvement and without building educators' knowledge of families' histories, literacy practices, and aspirations for their children. When educators have such knowledge, they begin to position students as learners with experiences that enrich their academic progress (Risko & Walker-Dalhouse, 2012). Communication with families must be two-way, with educators valuing families' involvement and families' understanding and supporting goals for instruction and providing feedback about their children's engagement. Part of the process for educators is learning about the family composition (e.g., extended members as part of nuclear family, single-parent families, two-mother or two-father families), family traditions and culture, and family literacy practices (e.g., story reading is replaced with multiple literacy-type games, songs, and dramatic play) so that realistic connections are made between school activities and students' lives, histories, and interests (Gregory, Long, & Volk, 2004; Mui & Anderson, 2008).

What steps should we follow? Implementing a family literacy study group involves the following activities.

- *Identifying specific goals.* Establish what you want to learn.
- *Building knowledge.* Read professional texts (e.g., as with book study described in chapter 4) that provide strategies for engaging families in conversations about school and literacy and how to initiate and sustain conversations that are open and helpful to both you and the families.
- *Identifying potential challenges.* Perhaps your school has a history of parents' reluctance to attend school events. Examine reasons for this (e.g., work schedules that are not conducive to after-school meetings, parents' beliefs that their involvement will not be helpful) and identify strategies for offsetting these (e.g., arrange for flexible and informal meetings or phone conversations).
- *Discussing home visits.* Perhaps home visits are required by the school district, or this is an activity that you want to investigate further, discussing pros and cons.
- *Identifying opportunities to talk with families.* These may include phone calls, emails, dialogue journals, or potluck dinners at the school.
- *Creating a plan to collect information.* Methods might include structured interviews, journaling with parents once a week where you share school activities and parents share home activities, sharing of students' writing from the classroom and requesting writing that may be happening at home, sharing classroom and home photographs with brief notes describing what is happening, and sharing observations about favorite books or literacy activities at school and in the home.

- *Planning to meet with families.* Try to meet three to four times a year, with the goal of sustaining involvement.
- *Setting goals for two-way conversations.* Begin by inviting parents to share their observations of their children (e.g., interests, responses to school activities, home activities) and whether or not they perceive problems that you should address. Share your observations and samples of the students' work, and your instructional goals.
- *Emphasizing student strengths and discussing concerns.* It is important to start with and elaborate on strengths; too often parents hear only about the problems.
- *Asking for feedback.* If you are anticipating some changes in instruction or specific strategies that will involve their children, ask for feedback and suggestions.
- *Using what you know.* With team members, plan to continue family involvement.
- *Informing families.* Report back to the families frequently during the year, sharing notes and observations and inviting feedback and face-to-face conversations.
- *Reflecting on learning.* Ask "What did I learn?" "How will I use this information?" "What do I expect the outcomes of my applications to be?"

What is an example of this activity? Mui and Anderson (2008) describe how they implemented home visits to learn about their students' literacy practices at home. Teachers at their school, located in a working-class community in a large western Canadian city, had a long history of building relationships with their students' families. They describe what they learned about one student, Jenna, and her family.

During their home visits, they took notes, engaged in informal conversations and structured interviews, collected samples of students' writing, and observed multiple literacy activities (e.g., board and card games, often focusing on word study; stacks of workbooks used for practicing literacy skills and playing school; and videos of children's dramatic play). They learned that bedtime reading was not a priority but that sharing family songs and stories, enacting family dramas, and completing school activities were. The family was an extended family that included a grandmother, several aunts and uncles, and several part-time nannies—all of whom shared in childrearing and responsibility for literacy activities. All family members communicated in at least two languages, and, as Mui and Anderson (2008) reported, the children were thriving in school with their English language (as an additive language) and literacy achievements.

What can we learn from this example? This example demonstrates what can be learned from families about their literacy interests and activities and the roles family members and caregivers assume during daily events. Most importantly, it reminds us that literacy practices out of school are enriching and are highly variable. The more we learn about families and their experiences, the better prepared we are to make connections between the texts we read in class and our students' history, and we come to understand the importance of multiple forms of literacy (e.g., writing, dramatizations, role-playing) that can be accessed in school to enrich our teaching and our students' learning.

What are the challenges and implications? With increasing diversity represented among our students, it is important to think carefully about how we can best invite families to be partners in the education of their children. As the Mui and Anderson (2008) example illustrates, there is much to learn from home visits and conversations with families that can inform and enhance instruction. Knowing how to start the conversation is an issue we face when studying family literacy habits and expectations.

Sometimes the first step is simply to ask parents, "How can I help your child succeed in my classroom?" When we asked that question to parents of students who were experiencing reading difficulties, we learned that parents had very specific responses. For example, some parents asked how they should hold discussions around shared reading or viewing of favorite TV programs. We also learned that parents can bring other parents into group activities. One of our colleagues who taught 2nd grade learned from her families that they wanted to start a home reading program that was "an enjoyable family time." As families learned about their common interests, they began to meet after school, and parents had many suggestions for one another as to how to get started and how to sustain family interest. Some brought videos to share with each other, developed posters on which they listed story conversation starters, and came together during the year to share their progress. Initiating family literacy study groups can lead to multiple ways to engage families and build positive relationships.

Lesson Study

What is it? Influenced by practices known as *jugyokenkyu* in Japan, lesson study provides for a systematic examination of instruction and student learning during carefully planned and observed lessons. Lesson study generally involves a small number of colleagues (6 to 10) in shared lesson planning, observations of one another's teaching, discussion of observations and student data, and refining lesson planning for subsequent lessons. This process may have several iterations before teachers feel comfortable in moving forward with independent applications in their own classrooms.

Why would we use it? Lesson studies can have several outcomes. There is increased knowledge, both of content to be taught—as the planning occurs, knowledge of content deepens—and of instruction, and collegiality deepens, including trust in colleagues' advice. Connections are made to goals, motivation, and a sense of accomplishment (Lewis, Perry, & Hurd, 2004; Puchner & Taylor, 2006), and to improved lessons. Educators on the teams are engaged in a careful analysis of specific teaching methods and decisions guided by their own inquiry (Bocala, 2015). A "knowledgeable other," who could be a peer teacher, literacy coach, or outside consultant, helps teachers deepen knowledge with introduction of new content for instruction and/or focus post-observation analysis on students' learning and thinking (instead of just surface lesson issues such as time allocation for lesson parts) (Bocala, 2015).

What steps should we follow to implement it? Lesson study has several components.

- *Identifying lesson objective(s).* Focus on the content/academic language students will learn.
- *Building knowledge.* Individuals working alone or on two- and three-member teams identify readings related to content and language objectives and then come together to discuss the readings. The school's instructional leaders and literacy coaches could support the team's efforts in locating resources.
- *Generating a lesson plan.* The plan develops for the first lesson with teaching and student objectives, instructional methods, student assessments, and procedures for teachers' note-taking.

- *Choosing a demonstration teacher for the first lesson.* Typically a group member volunteers, with rotations among group members for subsequent lesson iterations.
- *Developing protocols for lesson observation and post-observation conversations.* These are aligned with goals. For lesson observation, protocols could focus on students (e.g., interactions, responses to instruction, displays of thinking and questioning), teacher decisions (how instruction is initiated, discourse, text choice), and procedures (e.g., time allocation, grouping arrangements). Post-observation protocols would focus on what was observed, an analysis of student work, and recommendations for changes.
- *Planning discussion cycles.* A pre-observation discussion is set for the demonstration teacher to review goals and decisions. During the post-observation discussion, the group shares notes, examines student work, and identifies what seemed to work well and what changes could be made in a subsequent lesson. Typically the demonstration teacher initiates the discussion by sharing his or her observations and what was noticed about student involvement and performance.
- *Revising lesson plan.* A second team member implements a revised lesson (either with the same or a different group of students). The cycle of pre-observation, observation, and post-observation analysis is applied again.
- *Teaching additional lessons.* More lessons are planned if needed.
- *Reflecting on learning.* Ask, "What did I learn?" "How will I use this information?" "What do I expect the outcomes of my applications to be?"
- *Inviting a knowledgeable outsider into the process.* Often it is helpful to invite a teacher, instructional leader/literacy coach, or university consultant to lead the process during the first iteration. The leader should be knowledgeable about the educators' goals and expectations.

What is an example of this activity? Jasmine Bankhead, a new principal at Chicago's O'Keeffe School of Excellence, describes her school's movement to inquiry-based professional learning through lesson study (Hanford, 2015). They invited Akihiko Takahashi of the Lesson Study Alliance in Chicago to explain the benefits of lesson study. The teachers began by generating questions about the Common Core standards. One group of three teachers focused on a 3rd-grade Common Core math standard for geometry that involved finding the area of a shape and moving their students from simple memorizing of the formula "length times width" that did not help their students apply the formula to real-world problems. First they read articles and consulted with the faculty of the Lesson Study Alliance. The research and preparation took almost 6 months, with "lots of meeting after school" (p. 16). On the first day, the demonstration teacher provided an overview of the lesson, with materials and procedures. This lesson had two changes from previous procedures: First, the teacher asked the students to explain their thinking as they measured the area of objects, and second, she called the group together once they had worked with the measures to generate arguments for their decisions and critique the reasoning of others. These procedures are consistent with Common Core standards that emphasize explaining data and forming arguments with supportive information.

What can we learn from the example? The post-teaching discussion focuses on instruction and student learning; it is not an evaluation of the teacher. Teachers report that they appreciate the specific feedback they receive because it helps them to make changes in their instruction, even small changes, that facilitate student learning. As one teacher reported, there is group learning with applications and specific feedback, and this approach is different from former ones where teachers were told what to do and then abandoned while "stumbling around" (Hanford, 2015, p. 16) back in their classrooms.

What are the challenges and implications? There are several challenges and implications associated with lesson study. First, as our example illustrates, lesson study needs to be well-grounded in knowledge-building activities, opportunities to reflect on new approaches, and how changes to instruction may be effective and tailored to teachers' and students' needs. Without a firm knowledge base, it is easy to slip back into comfortable modes of teaching that are less than effective and not directed toward the intended outcome.

Lesson study also needs to be well-grounded in the understanding that those involved are conducting research on their teaching—identifying specific questions and methods for data collection and opportunities to analyze even small changes and student performance, accompanied by a willingness to implement iterations of lessons that move them closer to intended outcomes. The process is time-intensive, with learning and refinement developing over time (i.e., it is not a one-time fix). It requires keen observations of teaching and analyses of data, and teacher willingness to adjust and modify instruction throughout the process.

MENTORED RELATIONSHIPS

As we think about our professional learning, there are times when we want to draw some specific attention to our own questions and teaching challenges, and the help we seek may go beyond what we are accomplishing within groups or other forms of professional learning activities. Two forms of mentored relationships—collaborating with a critical friend and with a literacy coach—can provide very specific and focused help with individual challenges and needs.

CRITICAL FRIENDS AS PEER COACHES

What is it? At a recent meeting with Robbie Mitchell, Executive Director of Academic Strategy and Operations for the Tennessee Department of Education, she reminded us that the most important coach for teachers may be the "teacher down the hall." One form of peer coaching involves choosing a peer as a critical friend. Colleagues chosen by teachers will most likely be both fair and objective, ask provocative questions (Costa & Kallick, 1993), and feel comfortable offering a balanced critique.

Why would we use it? A critical friend as a peer coach has several advantages that aid professional learning. We are choosing a colleague who is familiar with the context for the problems and questions we want to address. By choosing our critical peer, we take charge of our own learning, and in the process often establish long-term professional relationships (Baron, 2007). A critical friend can provide objective reasoning around causes of problems and potential solutions (Iliev, Ilieva, & Pipidzanoska, 2011) with outcomes that may be more substantial than what can be gained when working alone (Baskerville & Goldblatt, 2009).

What steps should we follow?

- *Choosing a critical friend.* Choice is based on teachers' knowledge of peers that comes from previous interactions during professional experiences. If choices are difficult to make, school leaders may sponsor peer coach–finding sessions in which 4 to 6 teachers meet a few times to discuss students' work or a videotaped lesson. Through this discussion of the artifacts, teachers are identifying common interests, experiences, communication styles, and compatibility.
- *Setting purpose.* Teachers should be explicit about goals for the collaboration, estimated time involvement, methods for providing support (e.g., examining student work, observing teaching), and ideas about how the peer coach can be most effective.
- *Keeping records.* Records could be in the form of notes taken by each participant or by discussions that follow an established protocol. Baskerville and Goldblatt (2009) suggest a protocol for both the critical friend (e.g., ways in which I was a critical friend today, questions I asked that guided thinking about different perspectives, ways in which I stimulated thinking) and the teacher collaborator (e.g., How was I supported? How did my critical friend's questions support my thinking? What information that we discussed will be useful for problem solving?).
- *Planning for analyses.* Build shared understandings of concerns and questions by discussing students' work or viewing a video of the teacher's instruction to lead analysis. Open-ended questions (e.g., What did you notice? Was there a particular line of questioning that seemed to be most useful for engaging students? How frequently did students engage? Were there opportunities for students to infer, build argumentation, and support their answers?) facilitate collaborative thinking.
- *Generating suggestions.* Following analysis, each teacher (starting with the collaborating teacher) shares interpretations of strengths, possible needs, and possible solutions. The critical friend provides constructive feedback and suggestions during the discussion.
- *Planning for several cycles of analyses and discussions.* This refines instruction.

- *Reflecting on learning.* Ask, "What did I learn?" "How will I use this information?" "What do I expect the outcomes of my applications to be?"

What is an example of this activity? Baskerville and Goldblatt (2009) provide an example of critical friends as teacher mentors. Delia, a critical friend, filmed a teacher's instruction during an agreed-upon time and then viewed it with the teacher. Questions focused on the teacher's goals, beliefs about instruction, and whether these goals and beliefs were evident during instruction. In the teacher's reflection on this discussion, she noted that some questions were "uncomfortable," but she valued the discussion because "it starts with me . . . examining my own way of doing things" (p. 217). Further, she indicated that the discussions helped her to refine her thinking and take the initiative of trying out new ideas.

What can be learned from the example? In this example there is a shared viewing of the video and the learning for both individuals that comes with the discussion. Alternately, the two could share in the analysis of student work or a transcript completed by the critical friend during a lesson observation. The discussion starts with the teacher's analysis and opportunities to generate interpretations and questions, a common procedure for inquiry collaborations. The critical friend asks additional questions, such as "Did you accomplish what you intended?" or "What didn't develop as planned?" to refine future instruction.

What are the challenges and implications? Critical friend relationships may be initiated informally between pairs of teachers who choose to collaborate to solve problems that are particular to their own questions and instructional choices, or they can be established as a more formal way for the district or school to engage professional learning. To succeed, careful planning is required, with attention to goal setting and purpose. Specific questions can guide this process, such as "Who is the critical friend and how is this person chosen?" "How can the school district facilitate good matches between colleagues?" "What are the expectations for both the teacher and the critical friend?" "Are there necessary preconditions for successful critical friendship?" "What can the school system do to help establish a climate of trust and effective support among colleagues?" Setting time aside for teachers to confer is important.

LITERACY COACHING

What is it? Literacy coaches can have multiple roles within a
school, but we are most interested in their role as mentors. Coaches
and teachers initiate their relationship to jointly address questions and
problems, and the mentorship is aimed to be responsive to teachers'
questions and needs. Teachers and coaches take on shared leadership
responsibilities, learning from each other in the process. Teachers
lead the discussion with their questions, observations, and visions for
change; coaches lead by responding to teachers' concerns and initiating opportunities for shared learning and implementing new instructional practices.

Within an inquiry model, literacy coaching is not a top-down process, where a school administrator or the coach identifies goals and
expected outcomes for professional learning. Instead, coaches and
teachers plan together the work they will undertake and the goals for
teacher and student engagement.

There can be questions about how the coaching process is initiated within an inquiry process: How do the conversations begin,
and if needed, how does explicit guidance by the coach occur within a collaborative framework? There is no one right answer to these
questions, as the process will develop differently for those involved.
However, there are some general guidelines that are useful for successful coaching to occur within an inquiry model.

- Conversations between teachers and coaches are easiest
  when coaches are viewed as trusted colleagues, critical friends
  who can support professional learning. Often, other forms
  of professional learning (e.g., as members of the same book
  study or lesson study group) have helped build trusting
  relationships, so going to the next step of requesting or
  accepting individual help occurs quite effortlessly.
- Coaches who participate with teachers in professional
  learning activities demonstrate their continuing interest in
  acquiring new knowledge and refining their assessment and
  instructional practices.
- Collaborative work should occur within collegial relationships.
  Collaboration and collegiality are mutually enabling features
  of co-planning that can impact change.
- Amid the conversations that occur, coaches need to take time
  to listen to teachers' needs and to how they analyze problems

and proposed solutions, as teachers usually generate good insights about what they need to do (Burkins, 2007).

In the midst of planning for changes comes the need for instructional demonstrations that offer new direction or insights. Mraz, Salas, Mercado, Dikotla, and Ni Thoghdha (in press), in their collaborations with literacy coaches in the United States, Peru, South Africa, and Oman, advise building knowledge through "shared teaching" events, instead of positioning the coach as the "knowledge provider" who tells rather than assists. The coach takes a nonevaluative role and joins in activities that might involve the coach and teacher observing each other's teaching, observing a master teacher in another classroom or school, and holding regular conferences with the coach asking exploratory (nonjudgmental) questions (e.g., What was your goal? Why did you try that strategy? What else might you have done? How did this instruction relate to your objectives and the Common Core State Standards? What are the students learning? What was problematic for some students?). Such questions evoke thought and reflection; too much "telling" by the coach can do just the opposite, closing down dialogue and collaborative thinking and planning.

Within a shared teaching concept, coaches can mediate teachers' learning gradually over time. Learning is shared, as both teacher and coach are knowledgeable—but movement is directed toward the coach's guidance in building new knowledge about literacy assessments and instruction. The coach becomes the guide on the side (Vygotsky, 1978), advancing teachers' learning within a cycle of explicit mentoring that includes explicit explanations, demonstrations that invite guided reflection, and guided applications (Risko et al., 2008). The coach provides explicit demonstrations with joint reflections and encourages teacher implementation with feedback, until the teacher is feeling ready to apply independently what is learned.

Why would we use it? Coaching that engages teachers in the examination of their own decisions and instruction can have the greatest impact on their own learning and on their students' academic gains (Garet et al., 2001). Literacy coaching involves the sharing of knowledge between teachers and coaches, who together bring a history and context to the dialogue. Both generate questions and interpretations of what is occurring in the classroom, as the coach nurtures development of new knowledge and effective practices. To be effective, this mentored relationship should be instructive and sustained over time (Cochran-Smith & Lytle, 2001).

What steps should we take?

- *Getting started.* Coaches begin the school year with a clear job description that is developed with the school's administration (Vogt & Shearer, 2016). Major responsibilities are assigned to supporting teacher learning. Time is needed for the coach to join some of the professional learning groups, and often the coach is a resource for these groups (e.g., by identifying professional texts for book study, recommending experts who might do lesson demonstrations, or leading the first round of lesson study).
- *Organizing for coaching.* Coaching that is personal and individual should be one-to-one; group meetings may occur at times to discuss common problems or for sharing experiences with new instructional methods. Time for coaching and collaboration is held steady, with assurances that the administration supports this role. Bean and Ippolito (2016) describe a dual approach when organizing for coaching: There is organization within the "system" that requires administrator support, alignment with curricular goals and state standards, and commitment to intensity and duration of coaching activity. At the coaching level, there is respect for the coaches enabling relationships with teachers.
- *Fostering dialogue.* Coaching may start with a general discussion of a teacher's perspective on what is effective and what are the troubling areas, followed by a more specific focus on student data or teaching decisions (for examples, see Figure 5.2). If student engagement during text discussions is observed, the teacher and coach may rate student performance (e.g., some student talk but non-specific about text ideas vs. multiple examples of student talk that focuses on text's key ideas and supporting details, Bryk et al., 2015).

The coach can take on various support roles by sharing interpretations of data or brainstorming instructional strategies (Mraz et al., in press). Coaching may also start with a look back at the needs assessment data and questions about each teacher's perspectives on the findings to determine if some of these, such as choosing appropriate and complex texts or teaching

Figure 5.2. Questions to Guide Collaborative and Individual Student Data Analysis

Analysis of Performance/Interests/Engagement

1. What are you learning from the students' data about progress during the designated time period? What are students' strengths? What are problems?

Conditions Contributing to Performance/Interest/Engagement Changes

2. What are the areas in which change in performance occurred? How do you interpret those changes?

Instruction and Changes

3. What forms of instruction are you implementing most often? What instructional changes have you made that seem to be productive? Problematic?

Next Steps

4. What changes will you make now? To succeed with these, what do you want to learn before implementing changes?

comprehension and critical thinking skills, remain as problems to be tackled. Bean and Ippolito (2016) recommend the use of discussion-based protocols, such as those that help teachers identify problems of practice and possible reasons before generating potential solutions. Discussion-based protocols (as illustrated in Figure 5.2) can help the teacher and coach examine students' work based on expectations and readjust instruction and/or the assignment.

- *Preparing for instructional changes.* Supporting teachers' need for instructional adjustments requires a conversation about the changes that might be needed, and identification of both the teacher's and coach's perspectives and recommendations. One way to address proposed changes is to plan a lesson jointly and discuss goals and procedural steps. The coach demonstrates assessment and instructional strategies that can be discussed, building knowledge of instructional applications.
- *Planning observations that are telling.* Both the coach and the teacher may be observed, with multiple methods for collecting observational data. These include descriptions of what

occurs, a focused recording of selected elements of interest (e.g., teacher questioning), or a record of the observer's interpretations or comments (e.g., "Great decision to choose that text." "I noticed that students were asking questions but not solving problems."). A descriptive form of recording data often is useful early in building collaborative relationships, as it leads to discussions and questions about what occurred (not evaluations, but "What was happening when you asked the opening question?"). If the school has lesson rubrics, these, too, could be used for collecting observational information.

- *Holding the difficult conversations.* Conversations about instruction can be viewed as negative and evaluative, suggesting that instruction is inadequate, even when coaches wish to share information and suggestions as supportive and helpful. One way to hold the difficult conversation about teaching is what Mraz, Kissel, Algozzine, Babb, and Foxworth (2011) call a conference discussion that has an inquiry stance. Detailed field notes written during the observation are discussed in the conference with a series of questions instead of statements—statements seemed to be evaluative, whereas questions elicited reflection and interpretations.

- *Reflecting at the end of each session.* The coach and teacher address the questions "What did I learn?" "How can I use that information?" and "What are the expected outcomes?" Here the coach guides reflections rather than evaluates, offering observations that can support deeper reflections.

- *Collecting data over time.* When new methods or changes to methods of instruction are implemented, it is helpful to monitor progress by collecting data over time. Perhaps these data report on daily student comprehension performance, or amount of teacher vs. student talk, or other information that explicitly addresses the stated goals. Then data conversations are focused and directed toward specific instructional changes that seem to be helpful and those that may need further attention.

What is an example of this activity? Mraz et al. (2011) are part of a collaborative team representing faculty from the University of North Carolina Charlotte and the Charlotte-Mecklenburg schools who are supporting literacy coaches and pre-K teachers. There are two major initiatives: Initially the focus is on the professional learning of coaches, and then there is support for the collaborative efforts of coaches and teachers. Early in the process coaches joined study groups and read professional literature in order to advance teachers' knowledge of early literacy teaching and learning, and to promote teachers' reflection. At the meetings, the groups shared what they learned with one another. This had two outcomes: Knowledge was distributed and coaches learned skills for enhancing teacher learning.

What can be learned from the example? The coaches' use of conference-centered discussions that are inquiry-based (i.e., where coaches share detailed notes taken during the observation and ask open-ended questions that elicit reflective thinking) moved the coach from an evaluator to a colleague. Differentiated coaching addresses teachers' individual (personal) needs. With joint planning and demonstrations conducted by the coach, specific questions are addressed and new forms of teaching are implemented.

What are the challenges and implications? The coaching we describe above has several conditions supporting its effectiveness, including the involvement of highly knowledgeable coaches (in both literacy content and mentoring abilities), administrative support, well-defined expectations for the coach as a teacher collaborator (and not teacher evaluator), and a climate of collegiality sponsored school-wide.

There are many types of professional coaching, but the form of literacy coaching we recommend has characteristics that align with *cognitive coaching* (e.g., Costa & Garmston, 2002), where coaches are not judging or evaluating teacher performance, but instead are engaged in dialogue and the examination of practices that may be effective for particular situations; with *differentiated coaching* (Kise, 2006; Vogt & Shearer, 2011), where coaches implement coaching strategies that are most responsive to the problems teachers are facing, and their questions and beliefs; and *mentor coaching* (Nolan, 2007) and *peer coaching* (Robbins, 1991), where experienced educators provide assistance to less experienced teachers.

Professional Learning Activities: In Review

We have now discussed seven approaches to professional learning, activities that can be combined or implemented independently, all of which address inquiry as a problem-solving process for professional learning. At this point it may be helpful to think back on the goals of each and how they might be implemented to address specific questions and problems. In Figure 5.3, we provide an *At-a-Glance* summary of the purpose, steps for implementing, examples, and benefits of these activities. We hope this table will be useful as you review the activities—so much to remember—and begin to map the characteristics and importance of each activity (and think about ones that may be most useful for the professional learning of you and your colleagues).

CONNECTIONS TO THE PRINCIPLES
OF EFFECTIVE PROFESSIONAL LEARNING

The Blue Falls pre-K–4 team had specific questions initially about how to choose and implement complex texts with young readers and writers. During their first year of professional learning, they engaged in book study groups and lesson demonstrations. These activities enabled them to deepen their questions and to focus more specifically on providing struggling readers and writers access to complex texts. They worked on building disciplinary concepts and finding methods for inviting parents into their learning process. About half of these teachers joined teacher research groups focusing on specific forms of instruction, such as strategies to engage close reading; others examined their instruction through the lesson study activities. These activities were pursued yearlong, with teachers reporting back to their groups on what they were learning and using in their classrooms. All developed family literacy study groups at their respective schools, and with the involvement of their administrators initiated home visits and family sharing nights. The activities were *intense, dynamic, situated,* and *substantive.* Additionally, six teachers requested additional and individualized, personal support from their literacy coaches to guide their use of data to inform their instruction. As demonstrated by the Blue Falls educators and the examples we provided in this chapter, building capacity for change to address needs requires a commitment to addressing the most difficult challenges we face as teachers.

Figure 5.3. At-a-Glance: Inquiry-Based, Collaborative Professional Activities

Activity	Purpose	Abbreviated Steps	Examples in Text	Benefits
Book Study (Chapter 4)	1. To build and share new knowledge through access to professional texts 2. Typically coupled with other professional learning activities	1. Form groups 2. Choose book(s) 3. Clarify expectations 4. Choose text(s) 5. Read text/designated procedures 6. Prepare for structured, focused group discussion 7. Distribute knowledge 8. Reflect on learning	Hermosa schools, multiple topics, including conferring with students, conducting inquiry lessons (p. 80)	Iterative cycles of book-reading engage teachers in learning about assessment and instructional methods, their rationale, different viewpoints, and flexible use
Lesson Demonstrations (Chapter 4)	To provide an example of an instructional event and an opportunity to question and analyze what is modeled, situated in a classroom	1. Set goals 2. Build shared knowledge through professional reading 3. Identify demonstration teacher 4. Conduct pre- and post-lesson discussions 5. Include cycles 6. Reflect on learning	An Oklahoma teacher's lesson on integrating reading and writing (p. 83)	Lesson demonstrations can serve as anchors for further study, and as foci for direct application of lessons in teachers' classrooms.
Teacher Research (Chapter 5)	To engage all processes of inquiry learning	1. Build knowledge through professional reading (research methods; content) 2. Generate specific questions for research 3. Investigate to find answers to questions (collecting and analyzing data) 4. Address validity and ethical issues 5. Reflect on findings 6. Invite knowledgeable others for methodology	James Rye's university partnership with a school to investigate students' gardening project (p. 93)	Multiple forms of data collection and opportunities for peer feedback and dialogue contribute to teachers' confidence in their own decision-making.

111

Figure 5.3. At-a-Glance: Inquiry-Based, Collaborative Professional Activities (continued)

Activity	Purpose	Abbreviated Steps	Examples in Text	Benefits
Family Literacy Study Group (Chapter 5)	To build knowledge about students' family literacy habits and parental expectations	1. Identify goals 2. Read texts to identify strategies for engaging families 3. Identify potential challenges and ways to offset them 4. Discuss home visits 5. Identify opportunities to engage 6. Create plans for collecting and analyzing information, reporting to families 7. Plan for conversations; ask for feedback 8. Reflect on learning	Mui and Anderson home visits (pp. 96–97)	Demonstrates what can be learned about family literacy histories and interests Affords connections between literacy practices in and out of school
Lesson Study (Chapter 5)	Systematic examination of carefully planned and observed lessons.	1. Identify lesson objectives 2. Build knowledge through readings related to content and language objectives 3. Plan lesson/lesson protocols/discussion cycles 4. Choose teachers 5. Implement iterative cycles, refine lessons 6. Reflect on learning 7. Invite knowledgeable others with experience	Chicago O'Keeffe School of Excellence, with focus on students forming arguments to support judgments (pp. 99–100)	Increases knowledge of content to be taught and lesson design, with careful attention to student participation and learning Focus is on research of teaching and refining instruction.

Critical Friends as Peer Coaches (Chapter 5)	Trusted colleagues offer a balanced critique of teaching and objective reasoning around causes of problems and potential solutions	1. Choose critical friend based on history of shared experiences/approaches 2. Set explicit purpose 3. Keep records 4. Plan for analyses 5. Generate shared suggestions 6. Plan iterative cycles 7. Reflect on learning	Baskerville & Goldblatt example of shared observations (p. 103)	Can provide substantial outcomes that are specific to teachers' questions and concerns
Literacy Coaching (Chapter 5)	Literacy coach as mentor to address questions and problems; guide changes	1. Establish mentoring role of coach/one-to-one 2. Creating dialogue 3. Prepare for instructional changes/joint planning/modeling and demonstrations 4. Shared observations 5. Hold difficult conversations 6. Reflect on learning	Mraz, Kissel, Algozzine, Babb, & Foxworth conference-centered discussions and shared teaching examples (pp. 108–109)	Coach's role is changed from that of an evaluator to a colleague who shares in learning and provides explicit guidance that is responsive to individual needs of teachers.

CONNECTIONS TO THE COMMON CORE STATE STANDARDS
AND OTHER STANDARDS-BASED POLICIES

Two features of professional learning that have the most impact on student learning are prolonged study of complex concepts to deepen knowledge (Yoon et al., 2007) and the careful study of the content of academic disciplines and how students learn that content (Doppelt et al., 2009).

The professional learning activities and the accompanying examples we provided illustrate how educators can learn about and implement new standards, such as the Common Core State Standards. The examples we describe above are particularly useful when designing the long-term engagement of teachers—they are generative, they are developed by teachers for teachers, and they are substantive. Literacy coaches, content area teachers, teachers from other districts, and outside consultants, such as nationally recognized educators and/or university research professors, may be valuable resources for developing new knowledge. Bringing in "outsiders" as collaborators and co-planners may be needed to provide substantial learning in new areas that school systems want to address. Such an approach should not be seen as inconsistent with an inquiry approach (Merriman, 2014), as these outsiders can increase a school district's ability to scale up professional learning outcomes. Additional resources may include webinars or online videos of lessons that are indexed to the CCSS (Merriman Bausmith & Barry, 2011).

Questions for Reflection

1. Visit websites such as *Teacher and Action Research* at gse.gmu. edu/research/tr/tr-action. What are the characteristics of these projects? Evaluate the material by asking questions such as: What were the takeaway ideas? Were there areas that you hoped would be addressed? How can you address your concerns in your own project? How would you address validity and ethical issues?

2. Choose one of the examples of professional learning activities, such as Mui and Anderson's (2008) example of home visits. Read the full article about this activity. What did you learn? How might you apply these ideas to your classroom? What changes would you make?

3. Think about the role of a literacy coach within an inquiry model of professional learning. If you are a literacy coach, how would you implement the procedures we recommend? If you are a classroom teacher, what role should you assume as a teacher-learner in a collaborative relationship with your literacy coach?

CHAPTER 6

Evaluating and Understanding Change

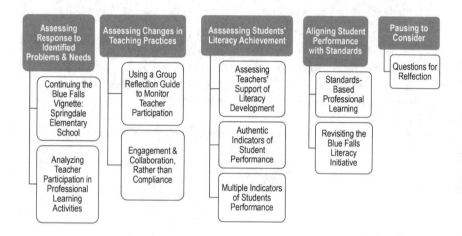

Throughout this book, our goal for effective and relevant professional learning is the transformation of instruction and improved student performance. As you consider Figure 6.1, notice how these questions have guided the development of each of the chapters. In this final chapter, we turn to the third section, Responding and Transforming.

Not surprisingly, all six principles for effective professional learning are relevant in this chapter. When evaluating the effectiveness and success of professional learning, we must consider the degree to which it has been *dynamic, intense, situated, substantive, collaborative,* and *personal*. As we stated in Chapter 1, it is the power of these principles, collectively, that is likely to have a sustained effect on *teacher learning*, which in turn leads to instructional improvements that ultimately impact *student learning*.

Figure 6.1. Professional Learning as an Inquiry Process

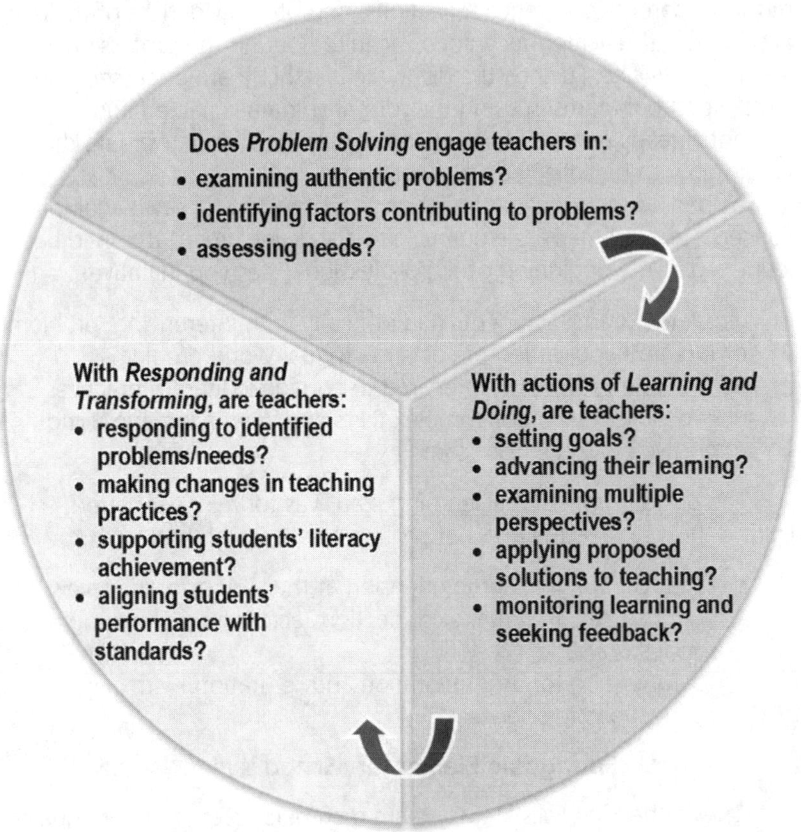

Does *Problem Solving* engage teachers in:
- examining authentic problems?
- identifying factors contributing to problems?
- assessing needs?

With *Responding and Transforming*, are teachers:
- responding to identified problems/needs?
- making changes in teaching practices?
- supporting students' literacy achievement?
- aligning students' performance with standards?

With actions of *Learning and Doing*, are teachers:
- setting goals?
- advancing their learning?
- examining multiple perspectives?
- applying proposed solutions to teaching?
- monitoring learning and seeking feedback?

Let's turn now to the Blue Falls vignette to see how the district literacy team and the school site teams collaboratively planned the ongoing assessment of their professional learning activities.

Connections to Instruction: Continuing the Vignette

Throughout the first year of the professional learning initiative for improving students' comprehension, the Blue Falls district literacy team worked with their schools on ongoing assessment of progress toward their goals. As part of the evaluation plan, they gathered and analyzed data about teachers' skills in teaching critical thinking, close reading, and writing. The literacy team members worked collaboratively with the teachers in their schools on organizing examples of lesson plans, journal writings, peer-mentoring observation notes, book study musings, parent conference reflections, and other evidences of their application of teaching techniques acquired during the professional learning activities. Further, the district leadership team discussed how to assist school teams in using the formative data collected about students' needs as a baseline for comparison to summative data that would now to be collected and analyzed.

As part of the process, the literacy team reviewed, once again, the concerns about Blue Falls students' literacy development that had been identified at the beginning of the professional learning initiative:

1. Across the grades, students had difficulty with inferencing, problem solving, and application of concepts to real-world problems.
2. Many students were not prepared to engage in literacy practices such as close reading of complex texts and identifying and using supportive evidence from complex texts.

The district professional learning plan was for a 3-year period. During this 1st year, the goals of professional learning had been to:

- Focus on building comprehension at the various grade levels, with text sets that make connections across literary writing and social studies.
- Teach writing for argumentation and refutation, with connections to science.

Springdale Elementary School's Plan

One of the Blue Falls literacy team members teaches at Springdale Elementary School, a building with 450 students in grades K–5. The school, with a culturally and linguistically diverse student body, has a free- and reduced-lunch program for 68% of its students, and 42% of its students are designated as English learners.

Issues that emerged from the analysis of the needs assessments completed by the teachers at Springdale at the beginning of the professional learning initiative included:

1. A lack of access to complex texts that are appropriate to the student population of Springdale;
2. A lack of confidence in providing appropriate comprehension instruction that focuses on critical thinking and close reading for students with varied language and literacy proficiencies; and
3. Selecting and teaching the academic vocabulary and academic language necessary for students to be successful while reading more complex texts.

During the school year, teachers at Springdale have been working together to tackle these issues. They have engaged in book study with two texts: *Pathways to the Common Core: Accelerating Achievement* (Calkins, Ehrenworth, & Lehman, 2012); and *Text Complexity: Raising Rigor in Reading* (Fisher, Frey, & Lapp, 2012). During their weekly meetings, they worked in Critical Friends as Peers groups (see Chapter 5), discussing their readings, sharing ideas and lesson plans, and mentoring one another. They also regularly shared their written responses to the book chapters, using argumentation and refutation, with evidence, whenever possible. Doing their own writing strengthened the teachers' confidence about teaching these important writing skills to their students.

In addition, a group of upper-grade Springdale teachers decided to investigate lesson study once they had read the books during the book study. (You will read more about this later in this chapter).

The Springdale Elementary teachers also shared data: monitoring data of their students' progress in reading increasingly challenging texts; language development data for English learners to determine vocabulary knowledge and growth; personal journal entries about success and challenges in selecting complex texts, attempting new ideas, and so forth.

Toward the end of the year, the teachers at Springdale Elementary were eager to see how they and their students were doing, given the challenging goals of increasing students' comprehension skills and strategies, and improving critical writing skills.

As teacher educators, we have, on occasion, taught university students who we believed were *born* to be teachers. They were intuitive and natural, they professed to loving children, and they claimed they knew that they were going to be teachers from their earliest recollections. Even so, and in support of the following quote by Ericsson and colleagues, these teachers needed guidance and supervised practice, not only in the beginning of their careers, but throughout if they were to become expert educators.

Consistently and overwhelmingly, the evidence shows that experts are always made, not born . . . the journey to truly superior performance is neither for the faint of heart nor for the impatient. The development of genuine expertise requires struggle, sacrifice, and honest, often painful self-assessment. There are no shortcuts. (Ericsson, Prietula, & Cokely, 2007, p. 1)

Throughout this book we have described a process for developing expertise in teachers through data-driven inquiry that is collaborative, goal-oriented, differentiated, and inclusive. Guided by the results of formative assessments of both students and teachers, goals were set and planning for subsequent professional learning was undertaken. The planning process included the views of multiple stakeholders, including students, teachers, parents, and administrators. Evaluating the effectiveness of the professional learning activities is the logical next step, but note that it is not a *final* step. Within an inquiry-based perspective, evaluation of professional learning is an ongoing and recursive process, whereby some questions are answered while others are generated. While some goals have been met, such as a particular group of students has made measurable progress, other goals remain the focus of continued professional learning, and at the same time, new goals may be determined.

The following section focuses on analysis of data and alignment of changes with the original goals for professional learning. We begin the discussion with the first question under Responding and Transforming, arguably one of the most important in this book.

ARE TEACHERS RESPONDING
TO IDENTIFIED PROBLEMS AND NEEDS?

In Chapter 1 we suggested that inquiry-based, collaborative learning will bring about shifts in teaching and learning. The third shift we listed proposes that those involved in inquiry and collaboration to improve teaching share an expectation that changes will occur and that these changes will be generated by the educators who have been involved in the planning and execution of the professional learning experiences. Further, it is expected that these changes will yield observable and analyzable data that may lead to additional changes in order to bring about desired results. In the past, when traditional professional development was undertaken, the people most concerned about observable data and analyzable outcomes were those planning and providing the professional development: administrators, supervisors, professional developers, university professors, and so forth.

However, with collaboration and inquiry-based professional learning, monitoring and evaluation become the responsibility of all those involved in the professional learning initiative, including those who are doing the teaching. Recall that in Chapter 3 we discussed procedures for developing needs assessments of both students and teachers. The purpose of these *formative assessment* data is to identify areas of strength and need, and to guide professional learning efforts. In contrast, *summative evaluation* data provide educators and stakeholders with information for making judgments and decisions about professional learning initiatives. A practical example of this difference is suggested by Guskey (2014a, p. 453): If I taste the cookie batter before I bake it, that's *formative*. When my guests eat a cookie, that's *summative*.

Within an inquiry approach, both formative and summative evaluation measures for teachers and administrators are predicated on a simple tenet: *When I'm the one asking the question, I'm more likely to be the one who wants to find an answer.* Certainly, rigorous standards provide direction to professional learning efforts, but it is teacher and administrator buy-in and commitment that bring about changes in instruction. Because monitoring is continuous throughout the professional learning experiences, the need for a high level of teacher buy-in and involvement is a given if anticipated changes are to be long-lasting, and buy-in is more likely when teachers are asking and addressing their own problems and questions. Further, levels of participation in and responses to the professional learning activities must be monitored on an ongoing basis so that modifications can be made early on in the process, if needed.

In Chapters 4 and 5, seven professional learning activities that are especially relevant for collaborative inquiry were described in detail: Book Study, Lesson Demonstrations, Teacher Research, Family Literacy Study Groups, Lesson Study, Critical Friends as Peer Coaches, and Literacy Coaching (see Figure 5.3). All were suggested as ways to involve teachers, administrators, school support personnel, and parents in working together to generate questions, identify problems, create goals, plan for instructional change, and then carry out recommendations in the classroom.

During these professional learning activities, determiners of success might include any of the following:

- robust, structured discussions;
- animated demonstrations of instructional techniques;
- shared writing through journals, lesson plan reflections, quick writes, book study responses, lesson observation notes, and so on;
- forthright dialogue about student performance;
- conviction among participants that they are heading in the right direction; and

- honest conversations about what is working and what is not, and what might need to be done to more finely hone literacy instruction for students.

These can all be indicators of the degree to which teachers are responding to identified needs through their buy-in with the professional learning initiative. And because this is a collaborative endeavor, school administrators' buy-in and involvement also need monitoring—principals who lack buy-in can derail professional learning experiences as quickly as, if not more quickly than, reluctant or resistant teachers.

ARE TEACHERS MAKING CHANGES IN TEACHING PRACTICES?

During conversations about teaching as related to the goals of professional learning, informal monitoring can take place through collaborative reflection of the entire group, or of peer mentors, literacy coaches, teachers, parents, and/or administrators. Too often, teachers attend a conference or training session, and come back to their classrooms to either implement, or not, whatever was taught at the workshop. Seldom does anyone ask the teacher what he or she learned, or what he or she is reflecting on after attending. These are missed opportunities, because teachers are more likely to make changes in an atmosphere of, "Tell me, what did you learn?" "What are you going to try with your kids?" "Why do you think that technique worked (or didn't work)?" "May I come visit your classroom and see (the new technique)?"

Collaboration and inquiry inspire sharing of ideas and techniques. Teachers' involvement and changing practices can be documented through reflection guides that can be used for a variety of the professional learning activities. For example, a literacy coach meets with teachers weekly during a book-study activity. Individually, the teachers and coach complete a reflection guide during their reading of the book that was selected by the group. Each week they come together to discuss the chapter they have read, and use their reflection guides to focus the discussion. The reflection guides thus provide information about teachers' levels of participation and involvement. See Figure 6.2 (pp. 124–125) for an example of a reflection guide used during book study by the teachers at Springdale Elementary School in Blue Falls.

You may have noticed that the Group Reflection Guide isn't so much about making sure teachers are reading the chapters as it is about getting questions, concerns, and hits and misses on the table so they can be discussed. When inquiry is both a goal and a by-product of professional learning, we are worried not so much about "compliance" as we are about sustained and productive *engagement*. In one of the books on professional development that we read in preparation for writing this book, two of the chapter authors suggested that "one of the most pernicious pitfalls [of professional development] is the perpetual problem of practitioner compliance" (Reutzel & Clark, 2014, p. 77). They also provide an interesting example of a research study on physicians' hand washing that was intended to lower infection rates in a hospital. Despite doing all sorts of things to make it easier and more efficient for doctors to wash their hands, and despite increasing the number of doctors who began regularly washing their hands, at the end of the study, the infection rates remained the same, because the percentage of doctors washing their hands never reached 100%. The percentage of doctors not washing their hands regularly before surgery apparently provided just the opportunity needed for germs and bacteria to multiply. It appeared that not all the doctors in this research study had buy-in, nor were they fully *engaged* in the efforts to decrease infection rates.

The Group Reflection Guide is one way for teachers to record and reflect on their participation in professional learning activities and the changes that they are making to improve instruction.

ARE TEACHERS SUPPORTING STUDENTS' LITERACY ACHIEVEMENT?

It is one thing to make changes in instruction by using new ideas and methods, but the real question is, do these changes support students' literacy achievement? After observing a teacher's lesson we will often ask, "Why did you select that particular activity for this lesson?" Sometimes we will get a response like, "Kids love it!" While it is great that students enjoy a particular activity, it is not really the response we are seeking. As an example, consider that a teacher's objective in a lesson is to have students posit an argument using evidence from a text. Including an activity like an oral debate or writing opposing headlines is a logical choice, given the objective of the lesson. In

Figure 6.2. Example of a Teacher's Reflection Guide for Springdale Elementary Book Study

Book Read: *Text Complexity: Raising Rigor in Reading* (Fisher, Fry, & Lapp, 2012)

Dates of Book-Study Meetings: Wednesdays, 3:15–4:30	Ideas Discussed Related to Close Reading	Teaching Ideas Tried	Student Reactions to and Results of Ideas Tried	Evidence That Ideas Worked or Didn't Work	Modifications Made to Ideas	Reflections
February 3	Ch. 1: Text Complexity is the New Black	Selected three books from classroom library; examined them for complexity	I read aloud a book that I thought would be complex; students were able to understand it okay during the read-aloud.	When students were asked to discuss the book's sequence of events in a group, many couldn't remember what happened, especially with much detail.	I don't know how to modify this idea yet.	I need to better identify what makes books complex for the students in my classroom.
February 10	Ch. 2: Quantitative Measures of Text Complexity	Used word-level analysis, sentence-level analysis, and Flesch-Kincaid Readability Formula to estimate readability levels of three different books in classroom library.	According to quantitative measures, the books that I thought were complex were really not. The sentences were relatively short and the words were pretty easy.	I asked three of my struggling readers to try to read the book that I'd measured for readability. All had difficulty with the book.	I selected what I thought was an easier book and measured it according to the quantitative measures. I then asked the same three students to read it. That book was too difficult, too.	I need to talk this process over with the book study group. When I first tried the quantitative analysis of the books, I thought it would be a good way to measure how difficult a book is. Now I'm not so sure.

Date	Chapter				
February 17	Ch. 3: Qualitative Measure of Text Complexity	I applied the qualitative measures to the same three books, and realized that not all books are "considerate," based on the criteria.	The text complexity rubric in the book helped me select a complex text in our basal that I had kids read; we had a good discussion about why it was challenging.	What's surprising is that even though most kids could read all the words and sentences, they had difficulty with the meaning because of some of the qualitative factors: for many, the text wasn't considerate.	Aha! I need to use both quantitative and qualitative measures when determining a text's complexity.	I think it would be helpful in our next book study group to read some text passages that are complex for us as adult readers. If we can talk through them and figure them out together, I think it would help us in teaching comprehension to our kids.
February 24	Ch. 4: Matching Readers to Texts and Tasks	Used the Checklist for Matching Readers to Text, p. 75, with several books from my classroom.	Based on the checklist, I matched two books with my most reluctant reader. Unbelievably, he picked one of the books to check out and take home.	My most reluctant reader came into the classroom and returned the book, saying he'd actually read it. We talked about it and I'm convinced he really read it.	The checklist is really long; I'm thinking I'll pull some of the key questions and maybe see if kids can use them themselves to select books.	Loved this chapter! Can't wait to talk about it with the others.
March 2	Ch. 5: A Close Reading of Complex Texts	Tried having kids use sticky notes while we did a close reading of an informational text.	Students always love using sticky notes, so we used them while reading an article about how sticky notes were invented.	Students were able to "mark" evidence in their text with the sticky notes. We could then discuss the evidence when I was asking text-dependent questions.	No modification needed; the idea worked great.	Still wondering how often we should try close readings so kids can become proficient with them.

Opposing Headlines, students partner to write two headlines about a particular topic from opposing perspectives. For example, consider these headlines that might be found in a newspaper or television report: 1) *Evidence Clearly Shows that Global Warming Is a Reality*; 2) *Historical Data Indicate the Earth's Temperatures Swing from Cold to Hot*. Students can write opposing headlines such as these and then use them for debate or discussion, and for writing news reports, while including supportive evidence from their research. With these activities, the teacher is supporting and developing her students' literacy achievement through the purposeful choice of an activity that clearly meets the lesson's objectives.

What follow are ways to use authentic artifacts to evaluate the degree to which professional learning has impacted teachers' support of students' literacy achievement. The ideas include both self-reports and classroom observations, and they yield multiple indicators of teacher change:

- *Reflective journals:* Teachers keep self-reflection notes during their participation in professional learning groups (e.g., book-study or teacher-research groups, lesson study), and about lessons in which they implemented techniques, methods, or approaches learned during professional learning activities. Of particular interest are reflections that are linked specifically to the school's inquiry questions and goals. Teachers are also asked to consider how the use of a technique or approach impacted the quality of a lesson, and how students responded to the techniques and approaches. Teachers can write to reflective prompts, such as:
  - » Did students appear to learn content more effectively when a different or new technique was used? How did you know?
  - » Did they retain the information during subsequent checks for understanding? How did you know?
- It's not enough for teachers to say they *used* a particular technique. Instead, the focus should be on *why* teachers used it during a lesson, and how it impacted student learning. When journals are used for conferencing with others (as indicators of professional growth), such as with an instructional coach, or during a presentation or discussion, they provide additional evaluation information about what a teacher has learned and applied in the classroom to improve literacy instruction.

Reflective journals are powerful tools that value teachers' insights into their own instruction, and, when shared with peers, they can motivate not only the writer but also those who are reading and discussing the author's reflections.

- *Peer observations*: Teachers invite other teachers (or just one "critical friend") to observe a lesson during which a technique or method is tried. If you cannot do this in person, set up your phone or a video camera to record a lesson. When both teachers are working on implementing a relevant technique or approach at the same time and they view each other's lessons, they can support and mentor each other through the process of improving instruction and analyzing student response. Bocala (2015) points out this benefit:

  > Relative to adults, sociocultural theorists argue that individual teachers learn through situated interactions with other teachers in their existing social relationship and communities of practice; that they are active agents in constructing knowledge; and that learning emerges through conversations and interactions among colleagues. (p. 350)

- *Portfolios:* Portfolios in teacher education have been around for decades (McLaughlin & Vogt, 1996), and they can have an important function in the evaluation of professional learning. By definition, portfolios are authentic, personal, situated, and "living" documents that illustrate, through multiple and diverse indicators, what a teacher knows and can do. In a portfolio, teachers can determine learning goals and provide evidence that they have attained these goals. Examples can include journal entries, Teacher's Reflection Guides (see Figure 6.2), videotaped lessons, lesson plans, book study, Group Reflection Guides, lesson study examples, coaching conference notes, and so forth. For each piece of evidence, the teacher writes why it is included and how it demonstrates knowledge and application of learning.

- *Administrative walk-throughs and informal observations*: In addition to the informal observations made by peers, it is important for administrators, supervisors, and coaches to also participate in the observation and conferencing process. If teachers are to change their teaching practices during and following professional learning, but no one regularly supports them through walk-throughs and observations, they may perceive that change is suggested, but not expected.

- *Structured conversations that address questions and/or professional learning goals:* Instructional conversations among teachers about a newly tried technique or method can yield interesting and useful information. Because the professional learning plan was developed around inquiry questions, it is important to determine if an adjustment in instruction, such as using a new approach, yields an answer to one or more of the questions. If so, why, and what is the answer? If not, why not, and what further adjustment might be needed to answer a particular question?

- *Satisfaction surveys:* While not the most important part of an evaluation plan, knowing whether participants enjoyed and felt they benefited from a professional learning activity is important, and it is an easy process to write a brief survey or questionnaire. Creature comforts such as a warm, inviting room with comfortable chairs do make a difference in terms of how we, as adults, learn.

When teachers are actively engaged in collaborative inquiry, and others on their team value their suggestions, insights, and questions (even when they are the tough ones to answer), they are more willing to try to change some of their teaching practices. In contrast, if educators are attending professional learning sessions simply because they are expected to be there, or they are held strictly accountable for doing something, the culture of the school is probably not one of collaboration, inquiry, and mutual support. We can best determine if teachers are making changes in their instruction by talking collaboratively with (not at) them, listening to them, observing them in a supportive setting, and validating their attempts to make positive changes, even if they're not always successful.

ARE CHANGES IN INSTRUCTION IMPACTING STUDENT LITERACY ACHIEVEMENT?

Very few studies of professional development report positive outcomes of students' achievement. In fact, Guskey (2014a, p. 448) reports that only 9 out of 1,343 studies published over a 20-year period were able to draw valid conclusions about the impact of professional development on student learning outcomes. Guskey reports further on several other studies, including two randomized field studies funded by the U.S. Department of Education, that yielded similar results.

In a study of 200 schools in Chicago (100 showing improvement, 100 not showing improvement), researchers found that those schools showing improvement had as a contributing factor high-quality professional development (Byrk et al., 2010). As we reported in Chapter 1, the research findings of Desimone et al. (2002) suggest that the following characteristics of professional learning lead to improving teaching practices: design or organization of the study; duration (contact hours over time); collaboration (as groups, not as individuals); features such as high engagement and active learning; alignment with a school's standards and goals; and a content focus (such as literacy). The assumption here is that improved teaching by teachers leads to improved learning by students.

The reasons are unclear why we have so little actual data about the impact of professional learning on student outcomes, but perhaps one reason why so few studies have been shown to positively impact student learning has to do with traditional professional development activities. For years, the prevailing model has been to have outside experts come into the school or district to teach everyone new instructional ideas or methods related to a particular topic or initiative. As dutiful teachers, we may have tried a new technique on Monday morning in our own classrooms, and perhaps we tried it several more times, improving how we used it with more practice. The problem was that someone else had decided that this was the technique or method we should be using. While it may have worked with our students, was it the most appropriate technique we should have been using, given our students' identified strengths and needs? And what did we learn from using the technique that afforded multiple applications and adjustments in order to sustain its use? Also, without support to make necessary adjustments, we probably didn't substantively change our instruction in a way that impacted our students' performance. So while we learned and tried the technique or method, we didn't sustain its use long enough or effectively enough to make a difference in the long run.

In contrast, within an inquiry-based model of *professional learning*, teaching techniques and methods are investigated and selected based on careful analysis of student assessment data. As you have read in earlier chapters, the type of professional learning that should be engaged in is that which will bring about the best instruction possible to improve, over time, student learning for a particular group of students. Therefore, the type of evaluation plan for determining the efficacy of a professional learning experience should also be tailored to particular teachers and students. Guiding questions for creating an evaluation plan for professional learning are suggested in Figure 6.3.

To provide context for these questions, let us use an example of lesson study as a professional learning activity. Having participated in lesson study for a period of time, a group of upper-grade teachers from Springdale Elementary in the Blue Falls District needed to ask what evidence they had that their application of the lesson study information in their classrooms was effective. In response, their evidence included weekly measures of students' critical thinking, reading, and writing skills, such as written responses to text-dependent questions about a piece of complex text; a debate during which students included argumentation and supportive evidence for positions they assumed; and opposing news headlines and accompanying articles that students wrote from different perspectives (Question 1 in Figure 6.3).

Given the regular and ongoing practice that students had with developing their critical thinking and reading skills, and many authentic indicators that demonstrated students were making progress,

---

Figure 6.3. Guiding Questions for Professional Learning Evaluation

1. How do we know whether or not the professional learning has been effective?
   a. What evidence do we have?
   b. What evidence do we need?
2. How do we determine whether or not anticipated changes are taking place?
   a. What evidence do we have?
   b. What evidence do we need?
3. What do we do if anticipated changes are not taking place, given the evidence we have? What modifications need to be made?
4. Should we continue with this initiative or discontinue it? Or should we continue with it, but only after adjustments are made?
5. How do we sustain what is working, give the evidence we have that it works?

---

the teachers anticipated at the end of the year that they would see students' standardized tests results indicating a positive gain (Question 2 in Figure 6.3). While some students demonstrated impressive gains, that wasn't the case for all students, so the teachers needed to determine for which students the lessons had been effective, and what, if any, adjustments needed to be made to provide more effective instruction and practice in critical thinking, reading, and writing skills (Question 3 in Figure 6.3). If adjustments to their lessons resulted in more students making progress, the teachers would probably continue with the modifications (Question 4 in Figure 6.3). At some point, the elementary teachers would either make lesson study a regular part of their ongoing professional learning, or they would have internalized it and it would become the way they taught (Question 5 in Figure 6.3).

Determining what is actually making the difference for students (or not), and why it is making a difference (or not), and what we need to do to continue making the difference (Question 3 in Figure 6.3), is where evaluation of professional learning becomes challenging. Using just one type of measurement (such as standardized test results) won't lead to deep understandings of how instruction and student outcomes are impacted by the professional learning. Instead, the use of multiple data sources is necessary in order to investigate the really thorny questions.

Using Multiple Data Sources

As with formative assessment, summative evaluation of change is enhanced when multiple data sources are used. You already have program goals and objectives derived from the formative assessment. For example, the Springdale Elementary upper-grade teachers in the previous example undertook lesson study to learn how to improve their students' critical thinking, reading, and writing skills. In the vignette's book-study example with some of the other Springdale elementary teachers, their focus was on improving their students' abilities to do close readings of complex texts. Using these similar goals, the teachers determined what information they needed (just as they did for the formative needs assessments), and how the data would be collected and analyzed.

One way to organize evaluation data is to use or adapt a system recommended by Guskey (2014a; 2014b). He describes five levels of evaluation, offering guiding questions for each, and suggests, specifically, how data (using multiple sources) can be gathered and analyzed, and how the resulting information can be used. The five levels of evaluation (Guskey, 2014a, p. 454) and some descriptive questions follow. Note that we have changed some of Guskey's questions to better reflect collaborative inquiry, and the types of professional learning activities that are discussed in Chapters 4 and 5.

1. *Participants' Reactions* (How did the participants feel about the particular professional learning? How well does the information relate to teachers' particular interests and students?)
2. *Participants' Learning* (Did participants acquire the intended skills and knowledge? Did the professional learning activity address participants' questions and needs?)
3. *Organizational Support and Change* (Were adequate resources provided? Was implementation facilitated and supported? Was success acknowledged? Was the professional learning appropriate for the original goals?)
4. *Participants' Use of New Knowledge and Skills* (Were participants able to apply what they had learned? Do indicators [the evidence] focus on participants' goals for professional learning?)
5. *Student Learning Outcomes* (How was student learning impacted? Were multiple indicators of learning outcomes observable?)

You can probably see that using the five levels to manage data for a summative evaluation plan would be helpful because there could be lots of data to collect and analyze. Whether you decide to use an existing structure such as Guskey's, or create one of your own, it will be necessary to consider how to select, use, and analyze multiple sources of data to see the degree to which teacher change has impacted student learning outcomes.

Student Change Data

One phenomenon that is really frustrating for teachers and administrators alike is when a school faculty works consistently, systematically, and conscientiously on a new initiative. Then, when student achievement is assessed, there is little or no positive change, and there even may be a measurable drop in achievement, before there is a move in a positive direction (Guskey, 2014a). This sometimes happens when there is a new reading or math program, new curriculum standards such as the Common Core, and/or new large-scale assessments.

Therefore, once again, multiple indicators are needed to adequately and fairly determine student-learning outcomes related to a professional learning initiative. Examples of diverse indicators of student achievement may include:

- Observation data from teachers
- Anecdotal records from teachers
- Student surveys or questionnaires
- Student records (cumulative records)
- Structured interviews of students, parents, teachers, and administrators
- Students' academic portfolios
- Examples of students' writing to specific prompts
- Results of follow-up reading assessments (e.g., *Basic Reading Inventory* [Johns, 2016], or *Qualitative Reading Inventory* [Leslie & Caldwell, 2016])
- Results of students' English language development, as measured by an appropriate English proficiency assessment (e.g., the WIDA ACCESS 2.0 for English Learners).
- School demographics and other records, such as academic comparison bands with other schools in the district.
- Standardized test results, especially related to observed trends (changes going up or down)

One factor that makes using student data challenging is that seldom does a school or district engage in one professional learning initiative at a time; in some cases, competing initiatives are undertaken, and this is problematic because it is virtually impossible to determine if one particular initiative has had an impact on student learning outcomes. Within inquiry-based professional learning, however, multiple initiatives would not be undertaken at one time. Instead, the inquiry more narrowly focuses a school's examination of an issue or problem. As an example, recall that in year one of Blue Falls' literacy initiative, everyone was working on improving comprehension and writing instruction, in particular critical reading and writing skills, across the grades and across the content areas.

ARE TEACHERS ALIGNING
STUDENTS' PERFORMANCE WITH STANDARDS?

Fortunately, this is one of the easier questions to answer during and following a professional learning initiative, because the entire initiative was developed around the literacy (or other content or language) standards. The beauty of using standards as a focal point is that the professional learning efforts are not diffused by attention to other topics or goals.

SUSTAINING THE PROFESSIONAL LEARNING EFFORTS

Roy (2014) suggests that to inspire change we must use continuous reinforcement in order to keep the momentum going. She also suggests a monitoring schedule of 30, 60, and 90 days after the inception of a professional learning initiative. We would add that we need to keep the end goal in mind—that of improving student literacy achievement, while supporting, validating, and reinforcing the educators who are making it happen. One of the biggest problems with sustaining professional learning efforts is that we in education are used to continual changes—we expect them; we even look forward to them. There is a prevailing attitude that if we do not like a particular initiative, it will move on and be replaced by something different, probably sooner rather than later. We see it happen when a school district's leadership changes and a new administration comes in with its own agenda, part of which is to replace what was going on under the leadership of the previous administration. We see it happen when an exciting new literacy approach appears, accompanied by a compelling book, great videos, wonderful trainers, and much attention. We see it happen when a professional journal article comes out with a new idea or method that sounds intriguing and interesting. Change gets us excited as educators, and excitement is a good thing. However, as you have read throughout this book, change needs to be focused and purposeful for it to be effective and meaningful.

Now we are not suggesting that once we have a good initiative in place it should stay in place forever. That would be foolhardy, because new research in education is always forthcoming and we need to be attentive and responsive to it. Within a collaborative, inquiry-based approach to professional learning, it's the collaborative inquiry that we want to sustain, rather than any one instructional technique, method, or approach. We continue to use what is working, as evidenced by improved student achievement, and modify or reject what is not bringing about anticipated results. The questions we ask and the research we do to find answers to them change; the process of inquiry-based professional learning does not. It remains robust, productive, and sustained because those involved in the inquiry process are the ones who care about it the most.

FINAL THOUGHTS

When we began working on this book, we could not have anticipated how much we would learn! Our research and writing process has truly been collaborative, inquiry-based, professional learning—and we learned a lot! Despite our many years as teachers and reading specialists, literacy professors, and yes, professional developers, when we began this project we entered a whole new realm of thinking and learning about what we all should be doing *with* teachers and administrators (not *for* them). In the beginning we were writing about good old PD, but before long we realized the paradigm was shifting under our feet (or keyboards, anyway), and we evolved in our thinking to *professional learning.*

If you have read this far, we hope you recognize that collaborative, inquiry-based professional learning offers so many more possibilities for exploring what makes effective instruction work in terms of improving literacy achievement for our students. You also have probably noticed that this is not a book full of a bunch of activities for teachers to try, and we purposely did not include what makes a really good professional developer or professional learning facilitator. The reason, of course, is that it is up to you and your colleagues to determine what activities you want to pursue, and with whom you'll be collaborating. The questions you ask, the research you do, the assessments you create and use, the instructional techniques you try and perhaps master—all are up to you and your colleagues.

As we conclude, we would like to share with you a quote from two of our colleagues and friends, Allison Swan Dagen and Rita Bean (2014). Please note that we substituted the term *professional learning* for *professional development.*

Professional learning is a journey, not a single event, and it is based on the belief that effective teaching can occur only when there are opportunities for ongoing and active learning. Such professional learning calls for teachers who understand and value the opportunity to continue to learn.

We wish you well on your own inquiry-based professional learning journey, and we hope that you find it to be rewarding, challenging, interesting, motivating, and fulfilling. Happy travels!

Questions for Reflection

As you consider the possibilities for collaborative, inquiry-based professional learning in your own school and/or district, consider these questions:

1. If you were in charge of initiating professional learning, who would you like to have as part of your collaborative team? Would you want only people who agree with your perspectives, or would you welcome diverse opinions? This is an important question, because in the "real world" of a school or district, multiple perspectives are the norm!

   a. What administrative and procedural structures need to be in place to begin a professional learning initiative?

   b. Will a funding source need to be identified?

   c. Are there key district people who need to be part of the team?

   d. What will the timeline be?

   e. Who will be the primary stakeholders?

   f. What role will language and literacy standards play?

   g. Who holds the "key" to student performance in the district? When should this person be brought into the conversation?

   h. What other questions should we be asking before we launch a professional learning initiative? Where do we find the answers to these questions?

2. You may have noticed that we did not have an ending to the vignette about the professional learning efforts in the Blue Falls School District. Because the Blue Falls literacy initiative is still in progress, as they turn to years 2 and 3 they will be continuing

their professional learning work, with new questions and activities. Given that their work is in progress, we ask that you draw on your experience and what you have been reading about professional learning to think about their potential student outcomes. If possible, have a conversation with a colleague (who has also read this book) about the following questions:

a. What do *you* think the results of the Blue Falls inquiry-based professional learning initiative were (and will be) after years 1, 2, and 3? Why do you think so?

b. Do you think Blue Falls educators completed their investigations about improving comprehension and writing instruction, and then moved on to study another topic? Why do you think so?

c. Or do you think the Blue Falls group continued their initiative, refining their search and clarifying their questions, as they continued to learn more about teaching critical thinking, close reading, and writing with purpose? Why do you think so?

3. What are your next steps?

References

Amos, J. (2014, June 9). Common Core and other state standards: New survey of School Superintendents Association finds optimism about new standards, but concerns about implementation. *Alliance for Excellent Education, 14*(11). Retrieved from all4ed.org/articles/common-core-and-other-state-standards-new-survey-of-school-superintendents-association-finds-optimism-about-new-standards-but-concerns-about-implementation

Atherton, J. S. (2013). Learning and teaching; Knowles' andragogy: An angle on adult learning. Retrieved from learningandteaching.info/learning/knowlesa.htm

Ball, D. J., & Cohen, D. K. (1999). Developing practice, developing practitioners: Toward practice-based theory of professional education. In G. Sykes & L. Darling-Hammond (Eds.), *Teaching as the learning profession: Handbook of policy and practice* (pp. 3–32). San Francisco, CA: Jossey-Bass.

Banilower, E. R. (2002). *Results of the 2001–2002 study of the impact of the local systemic change initiative on student achievement in science.* Chapel Hill, NC: Horizon Research.

Baron, D. (2007). Critical friendship: Leading from the inside out. *Principal Leadership, 7*(9), 56–58.

Baskerville, D., & Goldblatt, H. (2009). Learning to be a critical friend: From professional indifference through challenge to unguarded conversations. *Cambridge Journal of Education, 39*(2), 205–221.

Bean, R. M., & Ippolito, J. (2016). *Cultivating coaching mindsets: An action guide for literacy leaders.* West Palm Beach, FL: Learning Sciences International.

Birchak, B., Connor, C., Crawford, K. M., Kahn, L., Kaser, S., Turner, S., & Short, K. G. (1998). *Teacher study groups: Building community through dialogue and reflection.* Urbana, IL: National Council of Teachers of English.

Blank, R. K., de las Alas, N., & Smith, C. (2007). *Analysis of the quality of professional development programs for mathematics and science teachers: Findings from a cross-state study.* Washington, DC: Council of Chief State School Officers.

Bocala, C. (2015). From experience to expertise: The development of teachers' learning in lesson study. *Journal of Teacher Education, 66*(4), 349–373.

Bransford, J. D., Brown, A. L., & Cocking, R. R. (Eds.). (1999). *How people learn: Brain, mind, experience, and school.* Washington, DC: National Academy Press.

Burkins, J. M. (2007). *Coaching for balance: How to meet the challenges of literacy coaching.* Newark, DE: International Reading Association.

Byrk, A. S., Sebring, P. B., Allensworth, E., Luppescu, S., & Easton, J. Q. (2010). *Organizing schools for improvement: Lessons from Chicago.* Chicago, IL: University of Chicago.

Byrk, A. S., Gomez, L. M., Grunow, A., & LeMahieu, P. G. (2015). *Learning to improve: How America's schools can get better at getting better.* Cambridge, MA: Harvard University Press.

Calkins, L., Ehrenworth, M., & Lehman, C. (2012). *Pathways to the Common Core: Accelerating achievement.* Portsmouth, NH: Heinemann.

Callahan, R. M. (2005). Tracking and high school English language learners: Limiting opportunities to learn. *American Educational Research Journal, 42*(2), 305–328.

Carroll, T. G., & Foster, E. (2010). *Who will teach? Experience matters.* Washington, DC: National Commission on Teaching and America's Future.

Check, J. W., & Shutt, R. K. (2012). *Research methods in education.* Los Angeles, CA: Sage.

Cochran-Smith, M., & Lytle, S. L. (2001). Beyond certainty: Taking an inquiry stance on practice. In A. Lieberman & L. Miller (Eds.), *Teachers caught in the action: Professional development that matters* (pp. 45–58). New York, NY: Teachers College Press.

Costa, A., & Garmston, R. J. (2002). *Cognitive coaching: A foundation for Renaissance Schools.* Norwood, MA: Christopher-Gordon.

Costa, A., & Kallick, B. (1993). Through the lens of a critical friend. *Educational Leadership, 51*(2), 49–51.

Dagen, A. S., & Bean, R. M. (2014). High-quality research-based professional development: An essential for enhancing high-quality teaching. In L. E. Martin, S. Kragler, D. J. Quatroche, & K. L. Bauserman (Eds.), *Handbook of professional development in education: Successful models and practices, PreK–12* (pp. 42–63). New York, NY: Guilford.

Darling-Hammond, L., Wei, R. C., Andree, A., Richardson, N., & Orphanos, S. (2009). *Professional learning in the learning profession: A status report on teacher development in the United States and abroad.* Palo Alto, CA: Stanford University.

Desimone, L. M. (2002). How can comprehensive school reform models be successfully implemented? *Review of Educational Research, 72*(3), 433–479.

Desimone, L. M. (2011). A primer on effective professional development. *Phi Delta Kappan, 92*(6), 68–71.

Desimone, L., Porter, A., Garet, M., Yoon, K., & Birman, B. (2002). Effects of professional development on teachers' instruction: Results from a three-year longitudinal study. *Education Evaluation and Policy Analysis, 24*(2), 81–112.

Desimone, L. M., & Stuckey, D. (2014). Sustaining teacher professional development. In L. E. Martin, S. Kragler, D. J. Quatroche, & K. L. Bauserman

(Eds.), *Handbook of professional development in education: Successful models and practices, Pre-K–12* (pp. 467–482). New York, NY: Guilford.

Doppelt, Y., Schunn, C. D., Silk, E., Mehalik, M., Reynolds, B., & Ward, E. (2009). Evaluating the impact of a facilitated learning community approach to professional development on teacher practice and student achievement. *Research in Science & Technological Education, 27*(3), 339–354.

DuFour, R., DuFour, R., & Eaker, R. (2008). *Revisiting professional learning communities at work: New insights for improving schools.* Bloomington, IN: Solution Tree Press.

Echevarria, J., Vogt, M.E., & Short, D. (2017). *Making content comprehensible for English learners: The SIOP Model* (5th ed.) Boston, MA: Pearson.

Elish-Piper, L., & L'Allier, S. K. (2010). Exploring the relationship between literacy coaching and student reading achievement in grades K–1. *Literacy Research and Instruction, 49,* 162–174.

Elish-Piper, L., & L'Allier, S. K. (2014). *The Common Core coaching book: Strategies to help teachers address the K–5 ELA standards.* New York, NY: Guilford.

Ericsson, K. A., Prietula, M. J., & Cokely, E. T. (2007, July–August). The making of an expert. *Harvard Business Review.* Retrieved from hbr.org/2007/07/the-making-of-an-expert/ar/1#

Every Student Succeeds Act (ESSA). (2015). Reauthorization of Elementary and Secondary Education Act. Retrieved from ed.gov/essa

Firestone, W. A., & Mangin, M. M. (2014). Leading professional learning in districts with a student learning culture. In L. E. Martin, S. Kragler, D. J. Quatroche, & K. L. Bauserman (Eds.), *Handbook of professional development in education: Successful models and practices, PreK–12* (pp. 319–338). New York, NY: Guilford Press.

Fisher, D., & Frey, N. (2013). *Common Core English Language Arts in a PLC at work, Grades 3–5.* Bloomington, IN: Solution Tree Press; Newark DE: International Reading Association.

Fisher, D., & Frey, N. (2014). Effective professional development in secondary schools. In L. E. Martin, S. Kragler, D. J. Quatroche, & K. L. Bauserman (Eds.), *Handbook of professional development in education: Successful models and practices, pre-K–12* (pp. 205–228). New York, NY: Guilford.

Fisher, D., Frey, N., & Lapp, D. (2012). *Text complexity: Raising rigor in reading.* Newark, DE: International Literacy Association.

Fullan, M., & Knight, J. (2011). Coaches as system leaders. *Educational Leadership, 69*(2), 50–53.

Garet, M., Porter, A., Desimone, L., Birman, B., & Yoon, K. S. (2001). What makes professional development effective? Results from a national sample of teachers. *American Educational Research Journal, 38*(4), 915–946.

Glickman, C. D., Gordon, S. P., & Ross-Gordon, J. M. (2013). *SuperVision and instructional leadership: A developmental approach* (9th ed.). Boston, MA: Pearson/Allyn & Bacon Educational Leadership.

Goldman, S. R., Lee, C. D., Britt, A., Greenleaf, C., & Brown, M. (2009). *Reading for understanding across grades 6–12: Evidence-based argumentation for disciplinary learning* (USDE Grant No. R305F100007). Washington, DC: U.S. Department of Education, Institute for Educational Sciences.

Gregory, E., Long, S., & Volk, D. (2004). *Many pathways to literacy: Young children learning with siblings, grandparents, peers and communities.* London, England: Routledge.

Griffith, P., Plummer, A., Connery, L., Conway, S., & Wade, D. (2014). Successful staff development transforms writing instruction in an Oklahoma school. In L. E. Martin, S. Kragler, D. J. Quatroche, & K. L. Bauserman (Eds.), *Handbook of professional development in education: Successful models and practices, PreK–12* (pp. 521–527). New York, NY: Guilford.

Guskey, T. R. (2014a). Measuring the effectiveness of educators' professional development. In L. E. Martin, S. Kragler, D. J. Quatroche, & K. L. Bauserman (Eds.), *Handbook of professional development in education: Successful models and practices, PreK–12* (pp. 447–482). New York, NY: Guilford.

Guskey, T. R. (2014b). Using data in deliberate and thoughtful ways. In T. R. Guskey, P. Roy, & V. Von Frank (Eds.), *Reach the highest standard in professional learning: Data* (pp. 1–43). Thousand Oaks, CA: Corwin.

Guskey, T. R., Roy, P., & von Frank, V. (2014). *Reach the highest standard in professional learning: Data.* Thousand Oaks, CA: Corwin.

Hanford, E. (2015). A different approach to teacher learning: Lesson study. Retrieved from americanradioworks.org/segments/a-different-approach-to-teacher-learning-lesson-study/

Hattie, J. (2009). *Visible learning: A synthesis of over 800 meta-analyses relating to achievement.* New York, NY: Routledge.

Hiebert, E. H. (1983). An examination of ability grouping for reading instruction. *Reading Research Quarterly, 18*, 231–255.

Hord, S. M., & Tobia, E. F. (2012). *Reclaiming our teaching profession: The power of educators learning in community.* New York, NY: Teachers College Press.

Iliev, D., Ilieva, N., & Pipidzanoska, I. (2011). Action research democracy in mentoring schools. *International Journal of Humanities and Social Science, 1*(21), 58–65.

Johns, J. L. (2016). *Basic Reading Inventory—Pre-primer through grade twelve and early literacy assessments* (12th ed.). Dubuque, IA: Kendall-Hunt Publisher.

Joyce, B. R., & Calhoun, E. F. (2014). The school as a center of inquiry. In L. E. Martin, S. Kragler, D. J. Quatroche, & K. L. Bauserman (Eds.), *Handbook of professional development in education: Successful models and practices, PreK–12* (pp. 412–430). New York, NY: Guilford.

Kemmis, S., & McTaggart, R. (Eds.). (1988). *The action research planner.* Victoria, Australia: Deakin University Press.

Kise, J. (2006). *Differentiated coaching: A framework for helping teachers change.* Thousand Oaks, CA: Corwin.

Knowles, M. S. (1984). *The modern practice of adult education: From pedagogy to andragogy.* Wilton, CT: Association Press.

Kragler, S., Marin, L. E., & Sylvester, R. (2014). Lessons learned: What our history and research tell us about teachers' professional learning. In L. E. Martin, S. Kragler, D. J. Quatroche, & K. L. Bauserman (Eds.), *Handbook of professional development in education: Successful models and practices, PreK–12* (pp. 483–505). New York, NY: Guilford.

Learning Forward. (2011). *Standards for professional learning.* Retrieved from www.learningforward.org.

Leslie, L., & Caldwell, J. S. (2016). *Qualitative reading inventory* (6th ed.). Boston, MA: Allyn/Bacon/Merrill.

Lewis, C., Perry, R., & Hurd, J. (2004). A deeper look at lesson study. *Educational Leadership, 61*(5), 18–22.

Lick, D. W., & Murphy, C. U. (Eds.). (2007). *The whole-faculty study groups field book: Lessons learned and best practices from classrooms, districts, and schools.* Thousand Oaks, CA: Corwin.

Lieberman, A., & Miller, L. (2014). Teachers as professionals: Evolving definitions of staff development. In L. E. Martin, S. Kragler, D. J. Quatroche, & K. L. Bauserman (Eds.), *Handbook of professional development in education: Successful models and practices, PreK–12.* (pp. 3–21). New York, NY: Guilford.

Lucas, S R. (1999). *Tracking inequality: Stratification and mobility in American high schools.* New York, NY: Teachers College Press.

McDonald, J. (2001). Students' work and teachers' learning. In A. Lieberman & L. Miller (Eds.), *Teachers caught in the action: Professional development that matters* (pp. 209–235). New York, NY: Teachers College Press.

McLaughlin, M., & Vogt, M. E. (1996). *Portfolios in teacher education.* Newark, DE: International Reading Association.

Medrich, E. A., Fitzgerald, R., & Skomsvold, P. (2014). *Instructional coaching and student outcomes: Findings from a three year pilot study.* Annenberg Foundation, MPR Associates, Inc.

Merriman, J. (2014). Content knowledge for teaching: Framing effective professional development. In L. E. Martin, S. Kragler, D. J. Quatroche, & K. L. Bauserman (Eds.), *Handbook of professional development in education: Successful models and practices, PreK–12* (pp. 359–384). New York, NY: Guilford Press.

Merriman Bausmith, J., & Barry, C. (2011). Revisiting professional learning communities to increase college readiness: The importance of pedagogical knowledge. *Educational Researcher, 40,* 175–178.

Mraz, M., Kissel, B., Algozzine, B., Babb, J., & Foxworth, K. (2011). A collaborative professional development initiative supporting early literacy coaches. *NHSA Dialog, 14*(3), 1–11. Retrieved from dx.doi.org/10.1080/15240754.2011.586738

Mraz, M., Salas, S., Mercado, L., Dikotla, M., & Ni Thoghdha, M. (in press). Teaching better, together: Literacy coaching for English language teachers. *English Teaching Forum.*

Mui, S., & Anderson, J. (2008). At home with the Johars: Another look at family literacy. *The Reading Teacher, 62*(3), 234–243.

National Center for Literacy Education (NCLE). (2014). *Remodeling literacy learning together: Paths to standards implementation.* Washington, DC: Author.

National Governors Association Center for Best Practices & Council of Chief State School Officers. (2010). *Common Core State Standards for English language arts and literacy in history/social studies, science, and technical subjects.* Washington, DC: Author. Retrieved from corestandards.org/assets/CCSSI _ELA%20Standards.pdf

Neuman, S. B., & Cunningham, L. (2009). The impact of a practice-based approach to professional development: Coaching makes a difference. *American Educational Research Journal, 46*(2), 542–566.

Newmann, F. M. (Ed.). (1996). *Authentic achievement: Restructuring schools for intellectual quality.* San Francisco, CA: Jossey-Bass.

Newmann, F. M., King, M. B., & Youngs, P. (2000). Professional development that addresses school capacity: Lessons from urban elementary schools. *American Journal of Education, 108*(4), 259–299.

Nolan, M. (2007). *Mentor coaching and leadership in early care and education.* New York, NY: Thomson Delmar Learning.

Oakes, J. (1985). *Keeping track. How schools structure inequality.* New Haven, CT: Yale University Press.

Penuel, W. R., Gallagher, L. P., & Moorthy, S. (2011). Preparing teachers to design sequences of instruction in earth systems science: A comparison of three professional development programs. *American Education Research Journal, 48*(4), 996–1025.

Piper, W. (1930). *The little engine that could.* New York: Platt & Munk.

Puchner, L. L., & Taylor, A. R. (2006). Lesson study, collaboration and teacher efficacy: Stories from two school-based math lesson study groups. *Teaching and Teacher Education, 22*(7), 922–934.

Puzio, K., Newcomer, S. N., & Goff, P. (2015). Supporting literacy differentiation: The principal's role in a community of practice. *Literacy Research and Instruction, 54*(2), 135–162.

Raphael, T. E., Vasquez, J. M., Fortune, A. J., Gavelek, J. R., & Au, K. (2014). Sociocultural approaches to professional development: Supporting sustainable school change. In L. E. Martin, S. Kragler, D. J. Quatroche, & K. L. Bauserman (Eds.), *Handbook of professional development in education: Successful models and practices, PreK–12* (pp. 145–173). New York, NY: Guilford.

Reeves, D. B. (2011). *Finding your leadership focus: What matters most for student results.* New York, NY: Teachers College Press.

Reutzel, D. R., & Clark, S. K. (2014). Shaping the contours of professional development, PreK–12: Successful models and practices. In L. E. Martin, S. Kragler, D. J. Quatroche, & K. L. Bauserman (Eds.), *Handbook of professional development in education: Successful models and practices, PreK–12* (pp. 67–81). New York, NY: Guilford.

Risko, V. J., Roller, C., Cummins, C., Bean, R., Block, C. C., Anders, P., & Flood, J. (2008). A critical analysis of the research on reading teacher education. *Reading Research Quarterly, 43*(3), 252–288.

Risko, V. J., & Walker-Dalhouse, D. (2012). *Be that teacher! Breaking the cycle for struggling readers.* New York, NY: Teachers College Press.

Robbins, P. (1991). *How to plan and implement a peer coaching program.* Alexandria, VA: Association for Supervision and Curriculum Development.

Rohlwing, R. L., & Spelman, M. (2014). Characteristics of adult learning: Implications for the design and implementation of professional development programs. In L. E. Martin, S. Kragler, D. J. Quatroche, & K. L. Bauserman (Eds.), *Handbook of professional development in education: Successful models and practices, PreK–12* (pp. 231–245). New York, NY: Guilford.

Roy, P. (2014). Using data to make professional learning decisions. In T. R. Guskey, P. Roy, & V. Von Frank (Eds.), *Reach the highest standard in professional learning: Data* (pp. 44–77). Thousand Oaks, CA: Corwin.

Rye, J., Rummel, S., Forinash, M., Minor, A., & Scott, H. R. (2015). Garden-based learning: It's just the berries! Indoor and outdoor experiences engage students in plant science. *Science and Children, 52*(8), 58–68.

Sabers, D., Cushing, K., & Berliner, D. (1991). Differences among teachers in a task characterized by simultaneity, multidimensionality, and immediacy. *American Educational Research Journal, 28*(1), 63–88.

Sailors, M., & Price, L. R. (2010). Professional development that supports the teaching of cognitive reading strategy instruction. *Elementary School Journal, 110*(3), 301–322.

Santagata, R. (2009). Designing video-based professional development for mathematics teachers in low-performing schools. *Journal of Teacher Education, 60*(10), 38–51.

Sleezer, C. M., Russ-Eft, D., & Gupta, K. (2014). *A practical guide to needs assessment* (3rd ed.). Hoboken, NJ: Wiley.

Snow, C. E., Griffin, P., & Burns, M. S. (Eds.). (2005). *Knowledge to support the teaching of reading: Preparing teachers for a changing world.* San Francisco, CA: Wiley.

Steeg, S. M., & Lambson, D. (2015). Collaborative professional development: One school's story. *The Reading Teacher, 68*(6), 473–478.

Tschannen-Moran, M., & Chen, J. A. (2014). Focusing attention on beliefs about capability and knowledge in teachers' professional development. In L. E. Martin, S. Kragler, D. J. Quatroche, & K. Bauserman (Eds.), *Handbook of professional development in education: Successful models and practices, PreK–12* (pp. 246–264). New York: Guilford.

Tschannen-Moran, M., & McMaster, P. (2009). Sources of self-efficacy: Four professional development formats and their relationship to self-efficacy and implementation of a new teaching strategy. *Elementary School Journal, 110*, 228–248.

Umphrey, J. (2009, September). Toward 21st century supports: An interview with Linda Darling-Hammond. *Principal Leadership, 10*(1), 18–21.

Vogt, M.E. (1989). A comparison of preservice teachers and inservice teachers' attitudes and practices toward high and low achieving students

(Unpublished doctoral dissertation). University of California, Berkeley, CA.

Vogt, M.E. (2012). English learners: Developing their literate lives. In R. M. Bean & A. S. Dagen (Eds.), *Best practices of literacy leaders: Keys to school improvement* (pp. 248–260). New York, NY: Guilford.

Vogt, M.E. (2014). Reaching linguistically diverse students. In S. B. Wepner, D. S. Strickland, & D. J. Quatroche (Eds.), *The administration and supervision of reading programs* (5th ed., pp. 180–189). New York, NY: Teachers College Press.

Vogt, M.E., Echevarria, J., & Washam, M. A. (2015). *99 more ideas and activities for teaching English learners with the SIOP model.* Boston, MA: Pearson.

Vogt, M.E., & Shearer, B. A. (2016). *Reading specialists and literacy coaches in the real world* (3rd ed.). Long Grove, IL: Waveland Press.

Vygotsky, L. S. (1978). *Mind in society: The development of higher psychological processes.* Cambridge, MA: Harvard University Press.

Windschitl, M., Thompson, J., & Braaten, M. (2011). Ambitious pedagogy by novice teachers: Who benefits from tool-supported collaborative inquiry into practice and why? *Teachers College Record, 113*(7), 1311–1360.

Yamagata-Lynch, L. C., & Haudenschild, M. T. (2008). Teacher perceptions of barriers and aids of professional growth in professional development. *School-University Partnerships, 2*(2), 90–106.

Yoon, K. S., Duncan, T., Lee, S. W. Y., Scarloss, B., & Shapley, K. (2007). Reviewing the evidence on how teacher professional development affects student achievement (Issues & Answers Report, REL 2007-No. 033). Washington, DC: U.S. Department of Education, Institute of Education Sciences, National Center for Education Evaluation and Regional Assistance, Regional Educational Laboratory Southwest. Retrieved from ies. ed.gov/ncee/edlabs/regions/southwest/pdf/REL_2007033.pdf

Yoon, K. S., Jacobson, R., Garet, M., Birman, B., & Ludwig, M. (2004, April). Professional development activity log (PDAL): A new approach to design, measurement, data collection, and analysis. Paper presented at the annual meeting of the American Educational Research Association, San Diego, CA.

Youngs, P., & Lane, J. (2014). Involving teachers in their own professional development. In L. E. Martin, S. Kragler, D. J. Quatroche, & K. L. Bauserman (Eds.), *Handbook of professional development in education: Successful models and practices, PreK–12* (pp. 284–303). New York, NY: Guilford Press.

Zepeda, S. (2012). *Professional development: What works* (2nd ed.). Larchmont, NY: Eye on Education.

Index

NAME INDEX

SUBJECT INDEX

About the Authors

Victoria J. Risko is professor emerita, Vanderbilt University, and the 2011–2012 president of the International Literacy Association (ILA) (formerly the International Reading Association). She is a former classroom teacher and reading specialist, is the recipient of research and teaching awards, and is active as a professional learning facilitator and a speaker at national and international conferences. She was a member of ILA's Board of Directors, served on several IRA committees and commissions, and was President of the Association of Literacy Educators and Researchers and the International Book Bank. Vicki's research focuses on teacher education, reading comprehension, and meaningful learning, and uses of cases and multimedia environments to enhance learning, especially the learning of diverse and struggling learners. Vicki and her colleagues at Vanderbilt University are investigating the effects of *Translate*, an instructional method that engages students in the use of their first language to support reading comprehension of texts written in English. She is author/coauthor of articles published in *Reading Research Quarterly*, *The Reading Teacher*, *Language Arts*, and *Journal of Literacy Research*, among other journals and research handbooks, and is co-author of *Be That Teacher! Breaking the Cycle for Struggling Readers* (with Doris Walker-Dalhouse, Teachers College Press, 2012). In May 2011, she was inducted into the Reading Hall of Fame.

MaryEllen Vogt is professor emerita of education at California State University, Long Beach. MaryEllen has been a classroom teacher, reading specialist, special education specialist, curriculum coordinator, and teacher educator. She received her doctorate from the University of California, Berkeley. MaryEllen is an author of over 60 professional articles and chapters, and is co-author of 17 books for teachers and administrators, including *Making Content Comprehensible for English Learners: The SIOP Model* (5th ed., 2017), and the other books in the SIOP series. Her research interests include improving comprehension in the content areas, teacher change and development, and content literacy and language acquisition for English learners. MaryEllen has facilitated professional learning activities with teachers and administrators in all 50 states and in several other countries, including Germany, where she was invited to serve as a visiting scholar at the University of Cologne. She was inducted into the California Reading Hall of Fame, received her university's Distinguished Faculty Teaching Award, and served as president of the International Literacy Association (formerly International Reading Association) in 2003–2005.